CONSUMER PROTECTION IN NORTH-EASTERN INDIA

About the Editors

Prof. Ganga Prasad Prasain is currently Vice-Chancellor, Tripura University. Previously he was working as Dean, School of Social Sciences and Professor of Commerce in Manipur Central University, Imphal. Professor Prasain has worked as Head, Post-graduate Department of Commerce, Manipur University for thirteen years. He has completed his M.Com and Ph.D. from Banaras Hindu University, Varanasi. He has thirty one years of teaching and thirty eight of research experience at post-graduate level and seventeen years as Professor in Manipur University, Imphal. His area of specialization is Entrepreneurship Development, Human Resource Management, Marketing and Tourism Management. He has published seven books, seventy four research papers out of which ten papers have been published in International Journals.

Prof. Suresh Misra is currently Professor of Public Administration (Consumer Affairs) and Coordinator, Centre for Consumer Studies, at the Indian Institute of Public Administration, New Delhi. Before joining IIPA Prof. Misra worked as Professor of Public Administration with ATI Haryana, Haryana Institute of Public Administration, Gurugram.
Professor Misra holds his Master's in Political Science from Jawaharlal Nehru University (JNU), New Delhi, Masters in Human Resource Management from Pondicherry Central University, D.Phil. from Allahabad Central University and Diploma in Journalism and Mass Communication from Kolkotta.
Professor Misra has been associated with consumer studies for the last twenty five years and carried out a number of research and evaluation studies sponsored by national and international agencies. His pioneering study on Food Wastage in Social gatherings and a study on the Impact and effectiveness of the Consumer Protection Act during the last 25 years have been received very well. He has authored/edited 45 Books and contributed more than 100 articles/papers in books and reputed journals.

Dr. Sapna Chadah, Assistant Professor (Constitutional and Administrative Law), Centre for Consumer Studies, Indian Institute of Public Administration, New Delhi.
Dr. Sapna Chadah holds her Masters in Law (LL.M) from University of Delhi and PhD. in Law from Jamia Millia Islamia, Delhi. She has an experience of more than 15 years in the area of teaching, training, research and consultancy. Her major areas of interest include Constitutional Law, Administrative Law, Consumer Protection Law and Policy, Environmental Management, Laws in Urban Management, Regulation of Service Sectors and Privatization.
She has authored/edited 12 books, 7 monographs and contributed more than 25 research papers in journals of repute. She was associated with a number of research studies in the area of consumer protection and consumer welfare, Right to Information and Evaluation of various government schemes.

CONSUMER PROTECTION IN NORTH-EASTERN INDIA
Some Glimpses

Edited by
G.P. Prasain
Suresh Misra
Sapna Chadah

CONCEPT PUBLISHING COMPANY PVT. LTD.
NEW DELHI - 110 059

ISBN: 978-93-6344-563-5

First Published 2024

Published and Printed by

Concept Since 1974

Concept Publishing Company Pvt. Ltd.
A/15-16, Commercial Block, Mohan Garden
New Delhi-110059 (India)
T: +91-11-41101460
E: publishing@conceptpub.com, *W*: www.conceptpub.com

Cataloging in Publication--Courtesy: D.K. Agencies (P) Ltd. <docinfo@dkagencies.com>

Consumer protection in North-Eastern India : some glimpses / edited by G.P. Prasain, Suresh Misra, Sapna Chadah.

pages cm

Contributed articles.

Includes bibliographical references and index.

ISBN 9789363445635

1. Consumer protection--India, Northeastern. 2. Consumer protection--Law and legislation--India, Northeastern. 3. Consumer behavior--India, Northeastern. 4. Consumer education--India, Northeastern. I. Prasin, G. P. (Ganga Prasad), editor. II. Misra, Suresh, editor. III. Chadah, Sapna, editor.

LCC HC79.C63C66 2024 | DDC 381.3409541 23

भारतीय लोक प्रशासन संस्थान
Indian Institute of Public Administration
Indraprastha Estate, Ring Road, New Delhi-110002
www.iipa.org.in

Surendra Nath Tripathi, IAS (Retd.)
Director General
(Former Secretary, M/o Parliamentary Affairs, GoI)

Foreword

The modern world is world of consumerism. Consumers have access to goods and services available globally. The economic globalization, expanding transnational corporations, worldwide production chains, manufacturing outsourcing, etc. have made things difficult to comprehend for the consumers. This juxtaposes strong more entrenched business and weak consumers. With economic growth, consumers' purchasing power is increasing. The problem is further aggravated by wide gap between consumer expectations and lack of knowledge due to information asymmetry. India is one of the biggest consumer markets in the world but the question arises as to what extent consumer protection has kept pace with growing technological advancements. Manufacturers are exploiting consumers in the form of underweight and under measurement of goods, substandard goods and services, high prices, duplicity, adulteration and impurities, lack of safety devices, false or incomplete information, etc.

The increasing complexity of marketplace conditions calls for the need for consumer awareness. Knowledge and information about relevant product and service characteristics, existing consumer protection laws and possible channels of recourse is critical to making sound choices. Consumer awareness is the first line of defence against consumer problems. The consumer education is region specific as consumers' buying behaviour is affected by culture, geographic locations, urban lifestyles, way of using products, and many such factors.

The success of consumer movement mainly depends upon the level of consumer awareness generated in the country by educating the consumers about their rights and responsibilities, coupled with effective functioning of the consumer commissions where the consumers can ultimately assert their rights and seek redressal. Where the literacy rate is high and social awareness is greater, the consumer cannot be easily exploited. Within India, the level of consumer awareness varies from State to State depending upon the level of literacy and the social awareness of the people.

India's north-east which is known for its tropical rain forests, tribal cultures and handicrafts, tea, flaming and hot peppers, is slowly emerging as a magnet for business. With rapid economic growth in the region and increased purchasing power, the region is becoming an important market for business to capture. The book is an attempt to understand the consumer behaviour and preferences of consumers in north-east states. It also brings out the problems faced by the consumers' in the region and working of the redressal agencies in north-east India.

I congratulate the editors of the book for bringing out this useful volume which will provide a glimpse on the state of consumer protection and welfare in north-eastern states. I am sure the governments, policy-makers, researchers and readers, will find it useful and help them in understanding critical issues relating to consumer welfare.

Place: New Delhi
Date: 12 July 2024

Surendra Nath Tripathi

Preface

In a market driven economy consumers are the backbone of any business. Business starts with consumer and ends with consumer's satisfaction. Consequently, the welfare of consumers is an essential prerequisite for a healthy and sustainable economy. Confident, informed and empowered consumers are the engine of economic change as their choices drive innovation and efficiency. In spite of this the consumers are a vulnerable lot due to their continuous exploitation by the traders and the service providers. The consumers are being exploited by overcharging, black-marketing, rampant adulteration, short weights and measures, misleading advertisements, lapses in services offered dubious sale purchase agreements and other deceptive practices. A combination of new technologies and the globalization of economy, which have led to development of international trade and global competition, have further aggravated consumers' problems. It has led to vast expansion of business with a variety of goods and services to cater to the needs of the consumers which have left the consumers further confused and bewildered. In such a scenario the consumer protection is a socio-economic programme to be pursued by the government as well as the business as the satisfaction of the consumers is in the interest of both. In this context, the government, however, has a primary responsibility to protect the consumers' interests and rights through appropriate policy measures, legal structure and administrative framework.

No doubt consumer education and awareness is the most powerful tool to protect the consumer as only an educated, aware and alert consumer can make a rationale choice and protect himself against exploitation. Consumer Education is concerned with the skills, attitudes and knowledge required for living in a consumer society. It is inextricably linked to the basic skill necessary for living. An aware consumer not only protects himself against exploitation but induces efficiency, transparency and accountability in the entire manufacturing and service sector; thereby inducing a culture of good governance. One of the major problems facing the consumer movement in the country relates to lack of consumer education and awareness and North-eastern region is no exception.

The North Eastern Region (NER) of India, spread across the 8 States—Arunachal Pradesh, Assam, Manipur, Meghalaya, Mizoram, Nagaland, Sikkim and Tripura, is a captivating blend of natural beauty, rich cultural heritage and abundant natural resources. The region has diverse topographical and socio-cultural situation. The states have distinct cultures and multiple ethnic groups and are a fine example of unity in diversity. The North East region of India occupies strategic geo-political situation due to its international boundaries with Bangladesh, Bhutan, China, Myanmar and Nepal. North East India is thus strategically important. The region is bountifully endowed with bio-diversity, hydro-potential, oil and gas, coal, limestone and forest wealth.

Consumer movement in the North East is not very strong. The application of Consumer Protection Act, 1986 and 2019 remains unsatisfactory to a large extent. The Consumer Commissions receive very few complaints and the disposal is equally poor. There are many reasons for this poor state of affairs. The three-tier redressal mechanism lacks infrastructure and qualified manpower. There are very few programmes by the governments of North East states to empower consumers and take action against unscrupulous traders. Official apathy towards consumer protection is no doubt one of the major factors but lack of consumer education and awareness is equally important factor. North East states have international boarders and the supply of goods does not cover various safety, quality and standards. Moreover, consumers are unaware as to how and where to file complaints regarding products of foreign origin. Therefore, there is apathy towards consumer issues and problems. However, there is need to understand the problems and aspirations of the people of the region and accordingly policy and programmes need to be chalked out. The North East requires programmes that will empower consumers. The various stakeholders need to come together to take the consumer movement forward.

It is also a fact that no much study has been done on consumer movement in the North East. Therefore, this book fills the gap and presents a number of research papers on the state of consumer awareness and working of the institutional mechanism under the Consumer Protection Act in the North East Region. These provide some glimpses of the existing ground realities and what ails the consumer movement in this region of the country.

New Delhi
31 March, 2023

G.P. Prasain
Suresh Misra
Sapna Chadah

Contents

List of Contributors

A.S. Rapheileng, ICSSR Post Doctoral Fellow, Department of Commerce, Manipur University. **Email:** rapheilengas@gmail.com

Adaso Lophro, Assistant Professor Commerce, Dhanamanjuri University, Manipur. **Email:** adasolophro@gmail.com

G.P. Prasain, Vice-Chancellor, Tripura University & Former Dean, Department of Commerce, Manipur University, Canchipur, Imphal. **Email:** vc@tripurauniv.ac.in

Gopal Chetri, Principal, Sazolie College Kohima, Nagaland. **Email:** gopal123chetri@gmail.com

Huidrom Imobi Singh, Head of Department & Assistant Professor Economics, Don Bosco College, Maram.
Email: imobi.huidrom@gmail.com

John Mang Muan Lian Zou, Assistant Professor, Rayburn University, Assam. **Email:** johnzou13@gmail.com

Kangjam Mukhara Devi, Faculty Member, Centre for Entrepreneurship and Skill Development, Manipur University, Canchipur, Imphal. **Email:** mukhra.kangjam@gmail.com

Kh. Tomba Singh, Professor, Department of Commerce, Manipur University, Canchipur, Imphal. **Email:** kctomba@gmail.com

Kiirii Onand Monsang, Assistant Professor, D.M. College of Commerce, Imphal. **Email:** Onandmonsang@yahoo.co.in

Lalgoulen Khongsai, Research Scholar, Department of Commerce, Manipur University, Canchipur, Imphal.
Email: goukhongsai@gmail.com

Lalhriatchhungi, Research Scholar, Department of Commerce, Manipur University, Canchipur, Imphal.

Md. Kheiruddin Shah, Associate Professor (Retd.), D.M. College of Commerce, Imphal, Manipur.
Email: dr.khiruddinshah@gmail.com

Moirangthem Shanti Devi, Assistant Professor, Department of Political Science, Kha-Manipur College, Kakching, Manipur.

N. Tejmani Singh, Professor & Head, Department of Commerce, Manipur University, Canchipur, Imphal.
Email: drtejmani@gmail.com

P. Chinglen Singh, Research Scholar, Department of Commerce, Manipur University, Canchipur, Imphal.
Email: pchinglenakash@yahoo.com

Partakson Romun Chiru, Guest Faculty, Department of Management, Mizoram University. **Email:** mssmotbung@gmail.com

Ratan Kaurinta, Assistant Professor, Department of Commerce, Nagaland University, Nagaland.
Email: rkzeliang@gmail.com

Sapna Chadah, Associate Professor, Constitutional & Administrative Law, Centre for Consumer Studies, IIPA, New Delhi.
Email: sapnachadah@yahoo.co.in

Sharmila Thingbaijam, Assistant Professor, Department of Adult Continuing Education & Extension, Manipur University, Canchipur, Imphal.
Email: sharmila.thingbaijam@gmail.com

Suresh Misra, Professor, Public Administration (Consumer Affairs) and Coordinator, Centre for Consumer Studies, IIPA, New Delhi.
Email: drsureshmisra@gmail.com

Thangminlun Singsit, Research Scholar, Department of Commerce, Manipur University, Canchipur, Imphal.

Th. Binarani Devi, Principal, Thambal Marik College, Oinam, Manipur.

Thingbaijam Guneshwor, Manipur Institute of Management Studies (MIMS), Manipur University, Canchipur, Manipur.

W. Priyokumar Singh, Assistant Professor, D.M. College of Commerce, Imphal.

1

Introduction

G.P. Prasain, Suresh Misra and *Sapna Chadah*

The philosopher and economist Adam Smith in his work '*The Wealth of Nations*', has expounded that: "Consumption is the sole end and purpose of all production; and the interest of the producer ought to be attended to, only so far as it may be necessary for promoting that of the consumer."[1] Development coupled with increasing liberalisation and globalisation have resulted in the rapid economic expansion of world trade. The technological advancements have exposed the consumers to a new lifestyle and proliferation of human needs which have a great impact on the quality, availability and safety of goods and services. Further the convergence of economic, demographic, and technological forces have brought about unprecedented changes in consumer behaviour.

Consumerism is in fact a social movement seeking to protect the rights of the consumers in relation to the producers and providers of services. In its wider perspective it is an item on the agenda of administrative reforms for greater accountability, responsiveness, transparency and good governance. The importance and utility of consumerism and the concern for consumer care has considerably increased, perhaps, due to the change role of state as 'service state'. This demands that state and its sub-system must serve the people and that too with the best satisfaction. Satisfaction of the consumers generates confidence and in the confidence lays the credibility and respectability of the system.[2] Consumer protection has appeared in many facades and forms over the centuries. Governments' world-over have, from time to time, brought in legislative measures to cure the ills affecting the consumers. Consumerism has over the time developed into a sound force designed to aid and protect the consumer by exerting legal, moral and economic pressure on producers and providers of services.

The enactment of the Consumer Protection Act in 1986 was a milestone in the history of consumer movement in India. CP Act, 1986 was a unique and highly progressive piece of social welfare legislation providing for simple, speedy and less expensive remedy for the redressal of consumer grievances in relation to defective goods and deficient services. The Act provides effective, people-oriented and efficient remedy to consumers against unfair dealings and exploitation. The Act provides an alternative and additional remedy in the form of consumer commissions to the aggrieved consumers. The consumer can file a complaint before the three-tier redressal agencies for grievance relating to defect in product, deficiency in service, unfair trade practices and for excess price charged. Under the Act the Forums and Commissions can award suitable compensation besides other reliefs which is a distinct feature of the Act. The Act postulates establishment of advisory and adjudicatory bodies to safeguard the interests of consumers.

An effective, efficient and fair implementation of the 1986 Act was one of the conditions precedent for promoting the culture of good governance and thereby ensuring the better promotion and protection of the rights of consumers. The 1986 Act to some extent succeeded in bringing about fair play in the supply of goods and services and the consumer courts have played an important role in this. Certain degree of success was achieved in its 33 years of implementation and lakhs of people were benefited from it. But still there were deficiencies and shortcomings with respect to its operation which made it difficult for the consumers to get relief.

The rapid changes in the consumption pattern of the modern day consumer brought new challenges in the consumer movement of the country, which called for new approaches and strategies.

Buying myriad of products through online shopping is distinct feature of today's consumption. Ordering goods or services *via* the internet, making purchases using plastic money without paying in cash, consuming convenience foods or highly-packaged products without any food value are common these days. Consumers value goods which are cheap, convenient and time saving. With the advent in technology, digitization has become norm of the day. E-commerce, direct selling have redefined the market and provided a new dimension to consumer-seller relationship. Besides providing ease of transaction, these have also created newer challenges for the consumers to deal with and has made him more vulnerable. With these changes brought about by liberalization, globalization and digitalization, the 1986 Act failed to achieve desired objective of providing better protection to the interests of consumers.

The Consumer Protection Act, 2019

To meet the emerging challenges the Consumer Protection Act, 2019 had been enacted on 9 August, 2019. Barring few provisions, the New Act has come into force from 20 July, 2020 with government notifying Rules and Provisions like Consumer Protection Councils, Consumer Disputes Redressal Commissions, Mediation, Product Liability and punishment for manufacture or sale of products containing adulterant/spurious goods.[3] The rest of the provisions have come into force with effect from 24 July, 2020. The Consumer Protection Act, 2019 equips the machinery to meet the new emerging issues besides bringing efficiency in grievance redressal.

The CP Act, 2019 provides for a broader definition of consumer to include not only online transactions but also telemarketing and multi-level marketing which will impose responsibility at all levels. E-commerce has now been expressly defined under the Act of 2019 as buying or selling of goods or services including digital products over digital or electronic network. The Central Government on July 23, 2020 has also notified the Rules to regulate e-commerce entities. The definition of Unfair Trade Practices has been widened and unfair contracts have been defined and made as a ground to file complaint in consumer commissions. The Act provides for establishment of a regulator for the protection of consumer rights in the form of Central Consumer Protection Authority (CCPA). The new Act also has stringent provisions to deal with misleading advertisements.

The 2019 Act provides for simplifying the consumer dispute adjudication process, making it easier for the consumer to file complaints. The 2019 Act provides the option to file a complaint where complainant resides or usually works for gain. The Act also makes provision for e-filing of complaints. One of the major changes in the 2019 Act relates to the alteration of the pecuniary jurisdiction which existed under the 1986 Act and the manner in which the quasi-judicial fora at the District, State and National levels were to admit cases. Besides changing the pecuniary jurisdiction of the Consumer Commissions, the new Act also modified the formula for calculating the monetary jurisdiction. To simplify the adjudication process, Alternate Dispute Resolution mechanism in the form of Mediation has been provided in the new Act. The Act of 2019 has introduced Chapter VI on Product Liability which shall apply to every claim for compensation under a product liability action by a complainant for any harm caused by a defective product manufactured by a product manufacturer or serviced by a product service provider or sold by a product seller.

Consumer Awareness—Need and Importance

One of the major hindrances in the consumer movement in the country is the lack of awareness among the consumers. The consumers apart from being unorganized do not have the mechanism to understand their rights and responsibilities. Need for consumer education stems from the belief that education will reduce the need for institutionalized consumer protection;

the government laws to regulate non-competitive aspects of the market may not be needed as the consumer will be well equipped to determine whether he is at a disadvantage in the market place. Consumer education may correct this problem by showing them how to evaluate their needs and resources and then how to find the product that would best fit their requirements.

Consumers are currently in an increasingly complex market. With asymmetry of information and diverse array of products and services available in the market, makes things really difficult for the consumers to make a right choice. This necessitates that a system for accessing information is developed which provides convenience for consumers to obtain goods/services desired. At present the access to information is being used by sellers for unfair trade practices so that consumers become victims of dishonest promotions.

The Consumer Protection Act recognises six consumer rights which are: right to safety, right to be informed, right to choose, right to be heard, right to seek redressal and right to consumer awareness.[4] This was right to consumer education in the 1986 Act. The consumers lack education and awareness about their consumer rights. There are various incidents wherein consumer rights are getting violated; but many a times consumers are not even aware that their rights have been infringed and they suffer in silence. This condition shows that right to consumer awareness and education is crucial and steps in right direction by all the stakeholder need to be taken so that consumers do not experience losses.

North-eastern Region and Consumer Awareness

The North East India is a mosaic of geographical, ecological, and human diversities. In spite of such diversities, the region has some common features that clearly set it apart from the rest of the country. From times immemorial, North East India has been the melting pot of many communities, cultures and faiths. North East India comprises seven separate but adjoining states, as well as stand alone Sikkim. Arunachal Pradesh, Assam, Manipur, Meghalaya, Mizoram, Nagaland, Tripura and Sikkim are eight states located in the North East of the country. The North-eastern region is most beautiful tribal region of India. The region commands special importance for the country due to its strategic location and its cultural and historical uniqueness. The landscape, the range of communities and geographical and ecological divers these states quite different from other parts of the country. These North-eastern states are also referred as "eight siblings","eight sisters" or "seven sisters and one brother".[5]

The region is landlocked, surrounded by foreign countries—Bangladesh, Bhutan, China, Myanmar, and Tibet—with 99.5 per cent of international border and only 0.5 per cent of border with the country. The region is geographically isolated from the rest of India, because its only land link with the rest of India is through a narrow strip of land in the state of West Bengal.[6] These states cover an area of 2,63,179 sq. km, approximately eight per cent of the country's total geographical area and house around 3.76 per cent of the total population of the country.

Rich in natural resources and flora and fauna, the region is a gateway to East and South-East Asia. The NER has immense natural resources, accounting for 34 per cent of the country's water resources and almost 40 per cent of India's hydro-power potential. The NER is strategically located with access to the traditional domestic market of eastern India, along with proximity to the major states in the east and adjacent countries such as Bangladesh and Myanmar. The region is also a vantage entry point for the South East Asian markets. This resource-rich region, with its vast expanse offer tile farmland and huge untapped human capital, has the potential to be India's most prosperous.[7]

The separation of the region in different administrative units and presence of several tribes, languages, cultures and customs prevents them from being united. Ethnic conflicts between different communities and tribal group are common matter here. All the states of North East are marked by underdevelopment for various reasons. However, the region has great potential for contributing to the Indian economy. This region is blessed with natural resources and very much enriched with bio-diversity. Due to its strategic location (Gate Way to South East Asia) and scope of healthy economic relationship with neighbouring countries, this region could be one of the potential economic regions of India. Therefore, development and well-being of the people of the Northeast region (NER) is now receiving attention from the Government of India.

NER's key advantages lie in the agriculture and service sectors. The region has a strong comparative advantage in a variety of horticultural crops (fruits, spices) that are organic or near-organic. It also has a youthful, highly educated workforce, with high female labour force participation and proficiency in English, and a strong service sector orientation. This picture of NER is changing fast with the developments that have taken place in the past decade. There have been connectivity agreements with Bangladesh, accelerating infrastructure investments in region have all contributed to reduce the sub-region's economic isolation. In every state in NER, the average time to reach the nearest city has been cut from more than three hours in 2000 to one hour in 2015.[8] These developments in connectivity have ultimately contributed to lower the prices of great variety of products and reaped benefits for the consumers. Besides this the other developments internationally have also brought positive outcomes for NER. These include: growing incomes, leisure spending, and consumer awareness in India and neighbouring countries; a rising preference for fresh, healthful, safe, environmentally friendly, and socially responsible products; and the growing role of services in manufacturing, which is increasing demand for skilled resources.[9]

The North-eastern region is fast emerging as a magnet for upscale labels in consumer goods that are seeking to tap the growing demand in states such as Assam, Tripura and Manipur. From the makers of sports and fashion wear to branded jewellery chains, retailers are heading to the North East either to open their first stores or expand their presence. Rapid economic growth in recent years has increased the purchasing power of consumers in the region. Retailers are seeking to tap the demand in relatively unsaturated markets, eyeing new sources of revenue, after establishing themselves in the big cities. It is a brand-conscious and fashion-forward market. Growing incomes and rising purchasing power in urban areas of the North East are pulling consumers towards premium and branded products.

However, the main problem of consumers today is the low level of consumer awareness of their rights. The common man is becoming the target of exploitation of market forces due to lack of awareness, education, poverty, and ignorance. Therefore, consumer education has become very important since it is the only tool to protect the consumer. The chapter on 'Level of Awareness among Consumers in North Eastern States—An Assessment' by Suresh Misra & Sapna Chadah is based on research study undertaken to understand the level of awareness regarding consumer issues in the North East States of India. Four states, namely Assam, Manipur, Sikkim and Tripura were selected as sample to conduct the study. From each of these states two districts were selected to elicit consumers' perception on various consumer issues. The data were collected using a questionnaire to seek the opinions and views of the consumers randomly. Discussions were also held with the State Consumer Commissions, State Departments, peer leaders and also NGOs and the data is presented in this chapter.

21st Century epitomize the digital age. People of all ages and genre use mobile phones for various purposes like voice calls, video calling, e-mails, online shopping, social networking, entertainment, gaming, e-commerce etc. Purposeful use of the mobile phone provides the users with optimal service much beyond our imagination. Nonetheless, the haphazard use of mobiles can have severe negative impact on the life of young students' and people of all ages. Gopal Chetri & Ratan Kaurinta in their chapter on 'Behaviour of College Students' on Use of Cell Phone in Nagaland—A Case Study' have examined the impact of excessive use of mobile phones on the behaviour of younger generations. They have highlighted that in the present day, majority of the college going students use smart phones to remain connected with family, friends, for entertainment, gaming and social networking which eventually leads to wastage of most of their available time. As a consequence, many young people are losing track of their studies and mainstream activities of life. The precious time available in each individual's life can be profitably invested or wasted; depending on the type of activities they engage in. The widespread use of mobile phone by young age group for idling away their precious time can be attributed to the availability of cheap and affordable cell phones, ease of access to internet facilities alongside attractive data packages offered by nearly all the network service providers. To ensure judicious use of the time available by the college students, it has been argued that the policy makers devise a mechanism to stop these wide ranging exploitation of younger generation so as to transform the behaviour of students' towards a fair, educative and productive use of the available technology. If the same alarming and harmful behaviour is left unattended for too long, this menace might destroy the entire educational system causing a huge loss to the nation. This chapter is an attempt to study the behaviour of college students on the use of cell phone supported by the data collected from primary as well as secondary sources. The primary data are collected through personal interviews and questionnaire administered to 100 College students using convenient random sampling from Kohima district of Nagaland. The research study found that the college students who excessively use the android phones are the most vulnerable group of students to misuse the available e-gadgets and technology.

As economic globalization intensifies competition and creates a phenomenon of constant change, engaging and keeping customers has become all the more important. These days banks have realized that cost of attracting a new customer is much more than retaining existing customers, so banks are emphasizing more upon customer satisfaction. Customers prefer techno-savvy banks as well bankers and insist for top quality services and products served with minimum waiting time. The main problem today before the commercial banks, more particularly the public sectors banks, which were earlier operating in a sheltered regime after nationalization, is their long-run survival, tapping value customers and forging way ahead by retaining their valued customers. As endurance of the fittest has become the order of today, every bank is trying to persuade the best customer who is common for all. Retaining the existing customers and attracting new ones has become all the more difficult especially for public sector banks. People who are working in banks act as a bridge between the bank and the customer. They are the people who face customers directly and are the first ones to know what customer actually needs. As a service provider their role becomes very important in shaping bank's perception in customer's mind. As service can make or break a consumer, much emphasis is laid upon service delivery by most of the banks. The link between service quality and customer satisfaction has been subjected to concentrated scrutiny by a few service quality researchers. The chapter 'Customers' satisfaction pertaining to the banks of Manipur' by N. Tejmani Singh & P. Chinglen Singh attempts to make a relative analysis of level of customer satisfaction towards services provided by banks. The study has been conducted in Imphal city of Manipur and adopts an empirical analysis. This study concluded that private sector banks are preferred more by majority of the customers as they concentrate more on relationship building with their clients and are better equipped with modern infrastructure/facilities as compared to public sector banks.

Chapter by Huidrom Imobi Singh and Adaso Lophro on 'Consumer Welfare through Consumer's Equilibrium in Monopolistic Daily Newspaper Publishers in Manipur' analyses the consumer satisfaction achieved by reading the newspapers published in Manipur. Consumer is said to be in equilibrium when he gets maximum satisfaction from the consumption (reading) of various newspapers with the price paid for the same. There are four Newspapers in English and eight in Manipuri published in the morning and three in the evening in the Imphal area. The consumer satisfaction and fulfilment achieved by these newspapers can be analysed through simple micro-economics model and the use of demand and supply concept. The motive of the producers in today's competitive world is to provide satisfaction to the consumers and at the same time to make maximum profit as possible. On the other side, consumers are trying maximum satisfaction at a reasonable price. The finding regarding the price, consumer's contentment and producer's motive will provide useful information to the publishers, academicians, administrators and the consumers.

A consumer is a person who is buying goods for his personal use or consumption and not for any other purpose. The consumer has the right to choose any product according to his/her choice and services related with the product of his/her choice at competitive prices with assurance of satisfactory quality. With expansion of globalization, consumer culture is increasing with a high speed. Retailer, wholesaler, middleman and other in the production chain are taking advantage of this situation. Respective governments are responsible for the protection of the rights of the consumer within the framework of the Indian democratic norms. Manipur state government also takes care of the consumer rights by providing support and creating an environment for establishing a society that seeks to protect the rights of consumers and takes punitive actions against the unscrupulous traders and service providers. Manipur State Consumer Dispute Redrassal Commission is one of such organizations. Another important intervention for the protection of consumer's right is 'the State Consumer Helpline' which is functioning under the control of CAF and PD Department. In the name of the protection of the rights of the consumers, civil society organizations—student organizations, women, and lawyer groups are also agitating issues pertaining to consumer rights. This chapter on 'Consumer Rights and Government: Manipur Context' by Th. Binarani Devi examines the importance of the role of the government for protection of consumer rights to ensure better socio-economic development of the society. This chapter is based on both primary and secondary sources. These secondary sources which include related books, journals, Acts, Bills, resolutions, pamphlets, reports etc. have been analysed. The first-hand information has been collected through interview method based on fixed scheduled questionnaire. Generalization of the chapter will be made through induction method.

The chapter by G.P. Prasain & John Mang Muan Lian Zou on 'The Growth and Role of Consumer Disputes Redressal Commissions in India' aims at analysing the role and performance of the National Consumer Disputes Redressal Commission. The protection of consumers' interest has been one of the main priorities taken up by the Central and State governments in India since India's Independence. The emergence of the new consumer protection movement owes its origin primarily to the enactment and implementation of the Consumer Protection Act, 1986. The Consumer Protection Act, 1986 conceived a unique three-tier quasi-judicial consumer disputes redressal mechanism, with a District Consumer Disputes Redressal Forum (DCDRF) at the lowest level, a State Consumer Disputes Redressal Commission (SCDRC) at the middle level, and the National Consumer Disputes Redressal Commission (NCDRC) at the apex level. The National Consumer Disputes Redressal Commission is a quasi-judicial commission which was set up in 1988 under the Consumer Protection Act of 1986. For the purpose of the study, data have been collected and analysed with the help of secondary data from various sources, like books, articles, referred journal and websites.

Milk is one of the most nutritious foods for mankind. Milk production gives employment and at the same time generates revenue to the rural poor. This chapter on 'Consumption Behaviour of Liquid Milk in Imphal, East District of Manipur' by Lalgoulen Khongsai, A.S. Rapheileng, Kh. Tomba Singh, and Md. Kheiruddin Shah investigates the consumer behaviour of liquid milk in Imphal East District of Manipur. It studies the factors responsible for the influence of purchasing liquid milk and the relationship between different factors. The findings will be helpful for both the producers and consumers in making economic decision on liquid milk. The production and consumption pattern at the state and the national levels were analysed and it was found that there was a massive gap of difference in the consumption level. The average size of the family was found to be around five with an average monthly income of thirty thousand and consuming around one and half litres of milk daily. Correlation analysis indicated that there are no relationship pertaining to the respondents' size of family and income with their amount of consumption. There is great potential for liquid milk consumption in the study area and learning the factors responsible for consumption will give a massive boost in marketing liquid milk.

'Role of Educational Institutions in Consumer Protection in Manipur' by G.P. Prasain, Lalhriatchhungi and Kiirii Onand Monsang is an attempt to stress on the role of educational institutions in protecting the consumers and highlight the status of consumer protection and welfare in the state of Manipur. Consumers play a vital role in the development of a nation. Developments have made a great impact on the quality, availability and safety of goods and services but unfortunately the consumers are still victims of unscrupulous and exploitative trade practices. Many of us are not aware about how and where to file a complaint if a defective product is sold to us or there is deficiency in service or an adulterated food item is given. Here lies the importance of educational institutions in imparting education and awareness regarding the rights of the consumers. An aware consumer is an asset to the society.

By making people aware about their consumer rights, the schools and colleges may render their best contribution to consumer movement, which is yet to take concrete and viable status in the state of Manipur. The educational institutions can impart knowledge about consumers' rights among the students through various means. Including consumer protection as one of the subjects in the course-content at school level and in degree and diploma courses is one of the means to make the young consumers aware on their rights and protect themselves against any unfair trade practice. Besides this activities like training, seminar, talk show, competitions etc. can also be undertaken.

The chapter 'Consumer Protection in Manipur as per UN

Guidelines' authored by Moirangthem Shanti Devi, Kangjam Mukhara Devi and Thingbaijam Guneshwor tries to highlight the state of affairs of consumer protection in Manipur by comparing the current status of the state with the Guidelines on Consumer Protection by the United Nations (UN). Consumer Protection is a form of promotion and protection of rights of the consumers with an assembly of public and private provisions to ensure and improve the observance of the interest of the consumers. Direct protection is through regulating, monitoring and controlling by the nation's law; and indirect protection is through information and education of the consumers and support of the consumer associations. The first significant benchmark of consumer protection was embodied in the movement for rights of consumers which started in the 1960s, when J.F. Kennedy enacted the Charter of Consumer Rights on 15th March, 1962. The General Assembly of the United Nations Organisation adopted the "Guiding Principles for the Consumer Protection" which is a framework for the processing and consolidation of the policies and national legislation of every country regarding the consumer protection. Besides that it is also a stimulus for international cooperation.

'Need of Consumer Awareness: An Educated Person is not Necessarily an Aware Consumer' written by W. Priyokumar Singh and G.P. Prasain, highlights that in the modern world, consumers are the largest economic group in any country. But the consumers are not aware about the product, price, quantity, quality, hoarding and black-marketing the essential goods etc. and getting frequently cheated and exploited by the producers and sellers. In spite of the best consumer laws and serious measures of the government to protect the interests of the consumers, exploitation is increasing day by day. The major reason contributing to this situation is lack of awareness among the consumers about their rights and protection measures. The Consumer Protection Act is a compassionate social legislation that provides for protection of rights of the consumers and redressal of consumer disputes. So consumers particularly educated persons need consumer awareness about the product, i.e.

he/she consume the product. They should have correct information so that in case they suffer due to some defect or deficiency, they should be able to complain to the proper authority at right time for taking necessary action. Government of India has implemented various laws and measures to protect the consumers and amended the laws and regulations from time to time.

Consumer protection ensures that consumers receive information that will allow them to make informed decisions and are not subject to unfair and deceptive practices have access to recourse mechanisms to resolve disputes when transactions go away and are able to maintain privacy of their personal information. Now-a-day it is widely acknowledged that the level of consumer awareness and protection is true indicator of development of the country and progressiveness of civil society. The need of financial literacy in our country has gained importance because of low level of literacy and large section of population which is excluded from financial set up. Complicated financial products, low level of awareness and lack of knowledge about financial matters makes the want of financial literacy significant. Literacy skill always helps easily to solve the problem and builds confidence to claims and approach for their rights. The chapter by Sharmila Thingbaijam on 'Consumer Protection and Financial Literacy for Adult Learners' highlights that proper awareness is necessary among the rural people specially the adult illiterate about the consumer right for their social and economic development in the society. It also expresses that the importance of literacy, financial literacy always arises among the adult learners in particular and others in general which empower all to exercise the consumer protections and to use their roles and responsibilities to enhance the status of economy.

Manipur has gained popularity in sports and events; but it is equally famous and known for bandh and blockades too. The people have become too volatile and these collective activities have become general trend. Ignorance among the consumers of the state is main reason for the same. 'Dynamic Equation of Bandhs and Blockades and Challenges for Consumers in Manipur' by Partakson

Romun Chiru and Kh. Tomba Singh is based on a study initiated to determine the buying behaviour of consumers during bandhs and blockades in an un-organised market. It is still common practice that bandhs and blockades remain the favourite tool for exerting pressure on the state government. On the other hand, calculative businessman activity manipulates the consumers in terms of price, quantity and quality etc. Hence, keeping in view the vital goal of consumer welfare, grassroots level survey was initiated to observe, understand and analyse the behaviour of the rural consumers. A study were conducted at Bishenpur and Kangpokpi Districts; one from the valley districts and one from the hill districts in the state of Manipur. From each district, three development blocks were selected. An attempt was made to know the level of consumer buying behaviour during bandhs and blockades in the Districts. Using sampling techniques, 160 respondents from 32 villages were selected. The data were administered by using SPSS 21.0 version; the analysis shows that there is a strong positive relationship between bandhs and blockades and buying behaviour of consumers in Manipur.

Consumers play a vital role in the development of a country. An aware consumer is an asset to the society. The youth constitute nearly 40 per cent of the total population of India and it is important that they are educated. Education which is provided by schools and colleges and other institutions plays an important role as a facilitator of consumer awareness, consumer protection and consumer welfare. A customer becomes more conscious, aware and vigilant of his/her rights through the education he/she received. Before buying any goods or services, an educated and aware consumer asks and considers full information regarding quality and price of the goods and services, false and/or misleading advertisement etc. A numerous such reasons can be stated for role of education in imparting skills on consumer rights and welfare. Any dispute and redressal can be handled through education. The chapter on 'Role of Education in Consumer Awareness' by Thangminlun Singsit attempts to highlight the rights of consumer and the role of education in consumer awareness.

Notes

1. Smith, A., (1776). *An Inquiry into the Nature and Causes of the Wealth of Nations.* London: W Strahan, Book IV, Chapter VIII, vol. ii, para. 49.
2. S.S. Singh, (1991). "Consumerism: Concept, Concern and Consumer Care", theme paper, IIPA, p. 1.
3. Ministry of Consumer Affairs, Food & Public Distribution, (20 July 2020), Consumer Protection Act, 2019 comes into force from today, 4:53PM by PIB Delhi, https://pib.gov.in/PressReleasePage.aspx?PRID=1639925
4. CP Act, 2019 Section 2(9).
5. North East India—People, History and Culture, National Council of Educational Research andTraining, 2017, p. 5; North East —Indian Chamber of Commerce, https://www.indianchamber.org/states/north-east/
6. Kedilezo Kikhi, (2009), What Ails the North-East?: Challenges and Responses, *Sociological Bulletin*,Vol. 58, No. 3, pp. 346-366, Sage Publications, Inc., https://www.jstor.org/stable/23620663, accessed: 28-12-2019, 16:17UTCatp.346-347.
7. UN Priority Areas In India North-East, https://in.one.un.org/un-priority-areas-in-india/north-east/, accessed on 31 December, 2019.
8. Sanjay Kathuria and Priya Mathur, A Policy Framework to Build on Northeast India's Strengths, in Sanjay Kathuria and Priya Mathur (2020) (Ed.) Playing to Strengths -A Policy Framework for Mainstreaming Northeast India, The World Bank, p. 1 https://openknowledge.worldbank.org/bitstream/handle/10986/32740/9781464815058.pdf?sequence=2&isAllowed=y accessed on February 20, 2023.
9. *Ibid* at p. 1.

2

Level of Awareness among Consumers in North-eastern States

An Assessment

Suresh Misra and *Sapna Chadah*

Introduction

North East India was at the forefront of industrialization in the British India and was a thriving economic zone in the world. With the partition of the Indian Subcontinent in 1947, the North East became isolated, at least economically, from rest of India, Gradually, it surrendered to an inward-looking economic regime with broken transportation networks. However, the unique diversity, rich heritage and immense potential of North East have not been successful in making inroads into the enlightened era of economic development. Over the decades, when major parts of India have marched to the glory of economic development, North East has been left behind in the course of India's resurgent growth story. According to the Asian Development Bank (ADB), India's North-eastern states has suffered from a dearth of investment because of its remote, mountainous location, long distance from markets, high levels of poverty and unemployment, and limited private sector interest.

The cobweb of economic backwardness, frustration among youth, conflict of cultural and ethnic identities, mounting insurgency and government apathy to address the basic concerns of people in the region had made India's North East a cocooned island, where benefits of India's high growth trajectory have failed to trickle down. But in recent years, there has been a strong wind of change both in terms of private and public initiatives and in terms of projects heading towards North East which has the potential to uplift the poverty-ridden, exploited face of India's North-eastern states. Government initiatives: Under the 'Look East Policy' of Government of India, the Ministry of Development of North-eastern Region (DoNER) has been showcasing the strengths of North East to the neighbouring countries so as to set up new industries, attract foreign investments, boost tourism and enhance business and trade.[1]

The retail trade in North Eastern States is dominated by the unorganized sector. Especially, due to the geographical location, it poses challenges for the organized sector in expanding the business. Poor growth in transport and infrastructure are the major concern in the region for the development of organized retailing in the region. The region is lagging behind in poor railway transport system causing a high transportation cost. There are ample opportunities for the organized sector to grow in the region. Steps towards a better and efficient supply chain management would bring down the inventory cost, which can then be passed on to the consumer in the form of low pricing. Growth in the socio-economic and other indicators may pave the way towards development of organized retailing in the region. Investment from foreign sector has increased in the last couple of years but at a very slow rate. State government needs to look forward towards attracting foreign investment in overall development programmes as well as in retail trade. With the market set to grow strongly in the years ahead, domestic retailers are looking to expand fast.

Initial expansion plans of major retailers proved too ambitious and regulation prevented them in some cases from rolling out large-scale developments. Nevertheless, these investments have started to change in the retail environment. Reliance, Pantaloon and Bharti in particular, who have emerged as major players in many market segments, plough on with expansion plans across a wide range of formats. While there has been considerable expansion, retailers argue that there is still a lack of quality sites in urban locations. Boosted by growing demand, the retail sector should continue to grow rapidly, with the share of organized retail expected to double in the four years ahead, as growing middle class demands higher-quality shopping environment.[2]

One of the key economic impediments faced by the North East Region (NER) is lack of connectivity, largely on account of under-developed infrastructure. The lack of sub-structures including transportation, ICT and communications and market accessibility limit connectivity. Therefore, the region has been unable to develop in line with the rest of India or improve connectivity with neighbouring countries. To help these states utilize their potential, the Government of India adopted the 'Look East Policy' enacted in the early 1990s, which is now turned to 'Act East Policy'. In the course of imaging this region in a strategic sense, the 'North East Region Vision 2020' was unveiled in July 2008 with the aim of accelerating development to achieve sustainable progress and prosperity.

Large amount of monetary resources are being earmarked for funding developmental projects in the NER. A total of INR 53, 706 million (USD 8.9 billion) was allotted in the Financial Year 2014-15 for the advancement of the largely underdeveloped regions of North East India. Most of the Central Government ministries are compulsorily required to earmark 10 per cent of their budget for expenditure in the NER. Digital infrastructure is fundamental in supporting trade and community through information exchange and connecting people to people. It supports the delivery of services and reduces the cost of doing business, increases consumption and enhances operational efficiency. A number of initiatives are being undertaken by Government of India to enhance digital connectivity of the North East States. At policy level, new licences are being issued to telecom companies to raise coverage and introduce competition in the market. Business friendly policies are being introduced to encourage private bodies to build communities with hospitable environment and civic amenities. A community development roadmap to support future IT hub the region is being developed. Plan is to set IT Parks, high tech zones, food parks, ICT enabled educational institution, universities etc., the intuitional and infrastructural mechanism are also being built for enhancing digital connectivity.[3]

Now, the region is emerging as a magnet for upscale apparel and accessories labels that are seeking to tap the growing demand in states such as Assam, Tripura and Manipur. From the makers of sports and fashion wear to branded jewellery chains, retailers are heading to the North East either to open their first stores or expand their presence. The North East, home to a combined 45 million people as of 2011, comprises the states of Arunachal Pradesh, Assam, Manipur, Meghalaya, Mizoram, Sikkim and Tripura. Rapid economic growth in recent years has increased the purchasing power of consumers in the region. Fashion retailers making inroads into the region to tap consumers is a relatively recent phenomenon. Retailers are seeking to tap the demand in relatively unsaturated markets, eyeing new sources of revenue, after establishing themselves in the big cities. "It's a brand-conscious and fashion-forward market. Growing incomes and rising purchasing power in urban areas of the North East are pulling "consumers towards premium and branded products. To be sure, supply chain and logistics-related issues loom as potential challenges and scaling up may be a challenge given the limited density of population of cities in the region. The limited critical mass restricts the potential for new store openings."[4]

The main problem of consumers today is the low level of consumer awareness of their rights. The common man is becoming the target of exploitation of market forces due to lack of awareness, education, poverty, and ignorance. This potentially reduces the ability of consumers to protect themselves from unfair trade practices. Therefore, consumer education has become very important since it is the only tool to protect the consumer. Consumer education is one of the means to form skilled and conscious consumers towards their rights. Attitudes of consumers, ignorance, and laziness are the major factors which hinder information seeking by them. Being literate and educated and open to new ideas are not indicators of consumer empowerment. Consumers are empowered in real sense only when they know where to lodge complaint and become capable of submitting their complaints at the time of disadvantage and can assert their rights. Consumer empowerment can be promoted through government regulation and consumer education.

Government of India, Department of Consumer Affairs has taken a number of initiatives to generate awareness among the consumers in North-eastern states. To generate publicity in North-eastern states special campaign has been undertaken. The Doordarshan Kendras of North-eastern States ensure that the message reaches out in the local language. The audio as well as video spots were produced in the local languages specific to the North-eastern region such as Assamese, Khasi, Garo, Mizo, Manipuri and Naga. The AIR Kendras, the private FM channels and the newspapers having editions in North East region are being utilised for taking the campaign to the North East.

Statement of Problem

The Consumer Protection Act was enacted in 1986. The Act gives six rights to consumer and provides for a three tier redressal mechanism for resolution of consumer complaints within a period of three months or five months if product testing is required. The procedures are simple and the decisions are to be based on principles of natural justice. A consumer need not take the services of an advocate to file his complaints. The more the awareness about consumer issues and the related matters more the complaints are generally filed in the Consumer Fora and Commissions.

To understand the level of awareness regarding consumer issues a detailed study was undertaken in the North East States of India. There are eight North East states having similar geographical, social and cultural ethos. Four states, namely Assam, Manipur, Sikkim and Tripura were selected as sample to conduct the study. From each of these states two districts were selected to elicit consumers' perception on various consumer issues. The districts selected were Kamrup and Sonitpur from Assam, Imphal and Thoubal from Manipur, East Sikkim and Namchi from Sikkim and South Tripura and West Tripura from Tripura. The data were collected using a questionnaire to seek the opinions and views of the consumers randomly. Discussions were also held with the State Consumer Commissions, State Departments, peer leaders and also NGOs and the data is presented in this chapter.

Keeping in view the special conditions of North-eastern region a need was felt for a comprehensive study to assess the ground realities as far as consumer protection and welfare is concerned. It is in this context that the present study was undertaken by the Centre for Consumer Studies, Indian Institute of Public Administration, New Delhi to assess the level of awareness among the consumers and evaluate the working of the consumer redressal mechanism.

Objectives of the Study

The broad objectives of the study were to:

1. assess the level of awareness among consumers on various consumer issues;
2. evaluate the working of the Consumer redressal mechanism in North East states;
3. assess the measures taken to strengthen consumer infrastructure by the state governments; and
4. suggest recommendations to strengthen the Consumer movement in the North East states.

Methodology

The present study was an empirical research based on both primary and secondary data. It was a blend of both descriptive and analytical methods of study. The secondary data was collected from government publication, books, journals, newspapers and various prominent Voluntary Consumer Organizations working in this area. National information Centre (NIC) is major source of secondary data used in this study, from where CONFONET data were accessed.

The study looked at an area of situation providing information regarding institutional mechanism and its awareness among consumers which was gathered through primary surveys by using structured questionnaire among consumers. The questionnaire was subjected to reliability by pre-testing the constructed tools by administering it to 75 consumers randomly. The questionnaire was modified based on the responses from the consumers.

S.No.	Region	State	District	Sample size
1.	North East Region	Assam	1. Kamrup	75 respondents from each district
			2. Sonitpur	
2.		Manipur	1. Imphal East	
			2. Imphal West	
3.		Sikkim	1. East Sikkim	
			2. South Sikkim	
4.		Tripura	1. West Tripura	
			2. South Tripura	

Source: CCS Field Survey.

Sample Plan

The survey methodology adopted for the study was stratified random sampling. Everyone is a consumer hence target group is identified. Since India is a very heterogeneous country and having diverse geographic, socio-cultural and economic characteristic, a stratified random sampling reflects the characteristics of the population as a whole. 4 states from North East Region of India were selected for the study. These states were selected in a way that they can best cover geographical and demographical of the entire North Eastern region. These states were: Assam, Manipur, Sikkim and Tripura. From each state two districts were selected randomly for field study.

From each district 75 respondents were interviewed. The respondents from this district were selected by random sampling technique in a way that they can represent different socio-economic strata of both rural and urban area. Thus total sample of 600 respondents was taken for investigation. The data so collected was analyzed and tabulated. Appropriate statistical methods were applied to classify and analyze the data, collected on the subject. Discussions were held with various state government officials, consumer activists, academicians working in this area and NGOs.

One of the major drawbacks with the consumer movement is the lack of awareness and education among the consumers. This leads to various forms of exploitation of the consumers in the market. Exploitation is of various kinds like: food adulteration, deficiency in services, inferior quality of products, weights and measures etc.

Do Consumers Check Particulars before Purchasing Products?

For Consumer safety there are a number of measures that have been taken by the Government. One such measure is the Packaged Commodity Rules, according to which it is mandatory to make declaration about the date of manufacture, quantity, quality, expiry date, and manufacturer's details among other details. It is expected that an aware consumer will see these markings before making a purchase. MRP (Maximum Retail Price) is well known and is always checked by 64.4 per cent of the respondents, 11.2 per cent check them sometimes and 22.4 per cent of the respondents do not check the MRP written on the packed products. As far as checking the net weight/quantity of the packed product is concerned only 28.8

Table 2.1: Do Consumers Check Particulars before Purchase of Products

Particulars	Response	Assam	Manipur	Sikkim	Tripura	G.Total
MRP	Always	61.3	67.3	62.7	74.2	**66.4**
	Sometimes	11.9	14.3	11.5	7.0	**11.2**
	Never	26.8	18.4	25.8	18.8	**22.5**
Weight (Net content/Quantity)	Always	34.3	30.6	23.5	26.9	**28.8**
	Sometimes	40.8	46.0	65.5	50.6	**50.7**
	Never	24.9	23.4	11.0	22.5	**20.5**
Quality Mark	Always	15.0	6.3	2.5	13.1	**9.2**
	Sometimes	28.0	39.5	45.4	23.1	**34.0**
	Never	57.0	54.2	52.1	63.8	**56.8**
Manufacturing date and Expiry date	Always	22.7	23.9	56.3	26.3	**32.3**
	Sometimes	43.9	49.6	12.5	29.2	**33.8**
	Never	33.4	26.5	31.2	44.5	**33.9**

(Contd.)

Particulars	Response	Assam	Manipur	Sikkim	Tripura	G.Total
Veg/Non-Veg dots	Always	34.9	25.3	32.2	33.5	**31.5**
	Sometimes	50.2	45.8	39.7	43.9	**44.9**
	Never	14.9	28.9	28.1	22.6	**23.6**
Contents (Nutritional values)	Always	14.7	20.0	16.3	32.5	**20.9**
	Sometimes	47.1	35.5	32.7	42.0	**39.3**
	Never	38.2	44.5	51.0	25.5	**39.8**

Source: CCS Field Survey.

per cent always check it before purchase which 50.7 per cent check it sometimes and 20.5 per cent never check the weight/quantity of the product before purchasing.

9.2 per cent of the respondents always check the quality mark before buying a product while 34.0 per cent did it sometimes and 56.8 per cent of the respondents never checked the quality mark. Only 32.7 per cent always check the manufacturing and expiry dates written on the products. 31.3 per cent of them checked it sometimes. On the other hand 36.4 per cent of the respondents never check the manufacturing and expiry dates mentioned on the products. 31.5 per cent of the respondents always check the veg/non-veg details on the packed commodity, while 44.9 per cent check it sometimes and 23.6 per cent never check it. Contents are always checked by 20.9 per cent of the respondents which 39.3 per cent check it sometimes and 39.8 per cent of the respondents never check the contents mentioned on the product.

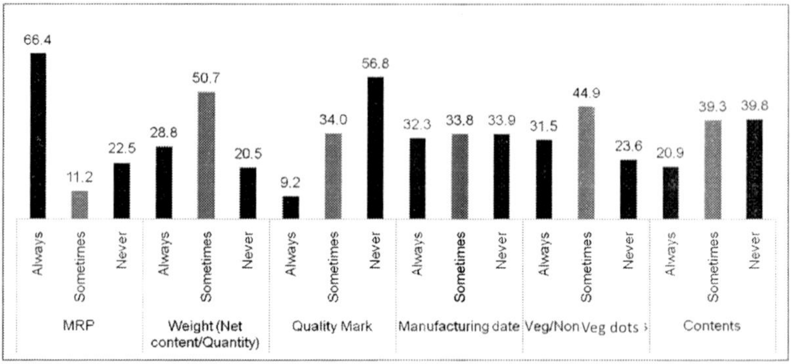

Fig. 2.1: Consumers Check Particulars while Purchasing Products

Source: CCS Field Survey.

Do Consumers Recognize Standard Marks?

Various Standard marks were shown to the respondents who were asked to recognize and name the standard mark. 64.1 per cent of the respondents could recognize ISI Mark as a mark of quality, while 35.9 per cent could not recognize. 79.1 per cent of the respondents did not know about hallmark. 83.6 per cent had never heard about FSSAI. 88.4 per cent did not know about AGMARK, 90.5 per cent did not know about BEE marking. 69 per cent of the respondents did not know about veg/non-veg marking. 92 per cent of them did not know about eco mark, 93 per cent did not know about recycling mark. The data shows that respondents lack awareness about standard marks which give them protection and ensures quality. ISI seems to be the most popular standard mark.

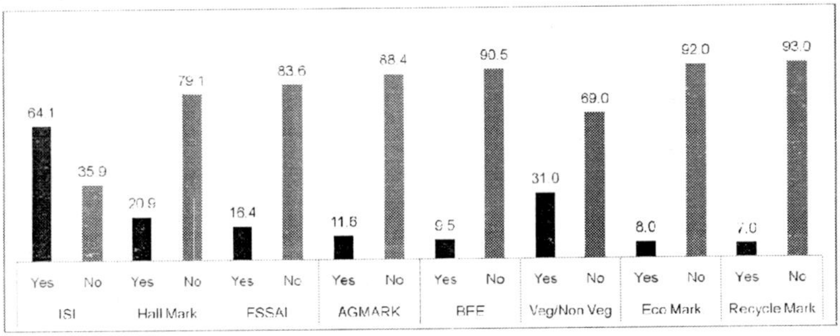

Fig. 2.2: Consumers Recognise Standard Marks

Source: CCS Field Survey.

Taking Bill/Receipt after a Purchase

The importance of an invoice and a bill is that it documents the services completed and/or products sold, along with the amount owned. The importance of the receipts is that it serves as documentation that the products and/or services have been paid for and the business transaction is complete. A bill is very useful if a consumer has to file a complaint against the defective product or deficient service. In practice many shopkeepers do not give bill and it is also true that many consumers also do not bother to take a bill.

Fig. 2.3 reveals that only around 11.63 per cent of the respondents ask for a bill/receipt always. 16.38 per cent of the respondents ask for the bill/receipts sometimes depending upon the value of the product or the service. However, 72 per cent of the respondents never ask or demand bill/receipt.

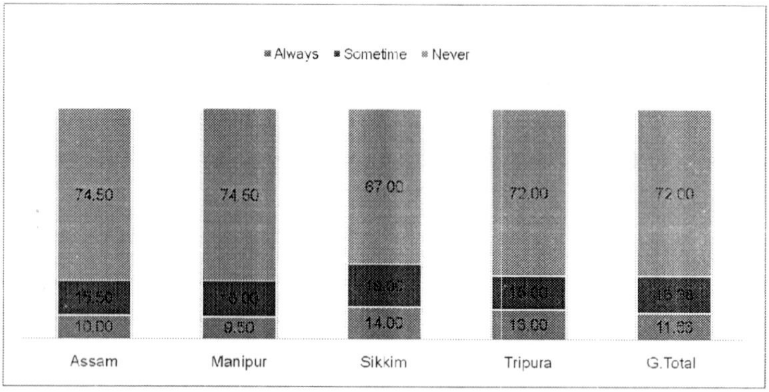

Fig. 2.3: Taking Bill/Receipt after a Purchase

Source: CCS Field Survey.

Consumer Experience Regarding Unfair Market Practices

The respondents were asked about their experience in the market on various kinds of unfair trade practices being followed by unscrupulous traders. 38 per cent of the respondents had an experience of food adulteration. Legal Metrology rules are being flouted in the market. Illegal weights like stones are still being used. Very few shopkeepers are using electronic weighing balance. As a result of this 60.3 per cent of the respondents had experienced less weight of the products that they bought. Charging more than MRP is a common practice both in urban and rural areas 72.8 per cent of the respondents had been charged more than MRP. As regards quality of the products is concerned, 39.4 per cent had got poor quality products. 37.0 per cent had experience of poor quality service delivery. 78.4 per cent of the respondents had not experienced any false in formations regarding quality of goods and services. Fig. 2.4 shows that various kinds of exploitation continue at the market place.

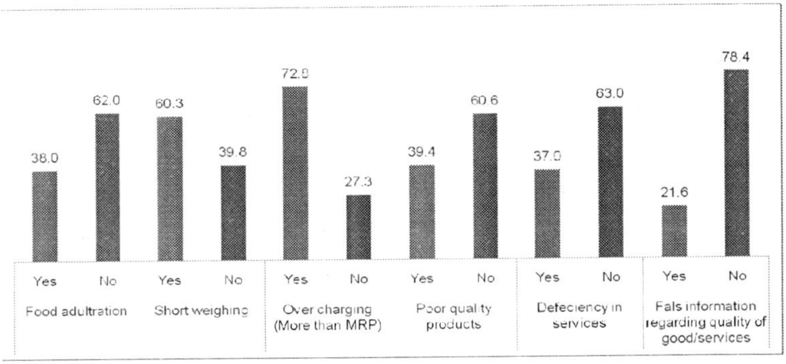

Fig. 2.4: Consumers' Experience regarding Unfair Market Practices

Source: CCS Field Survey.

Consumer's Action Regarding Experience of Cheating

It was also important to understand as to the action taken by the consumers in case of exploitation in the market. 25.5 per cent of the respondents did not take any action after being cheating in the market. On the other hand nearly 60 per cent tried to get the price

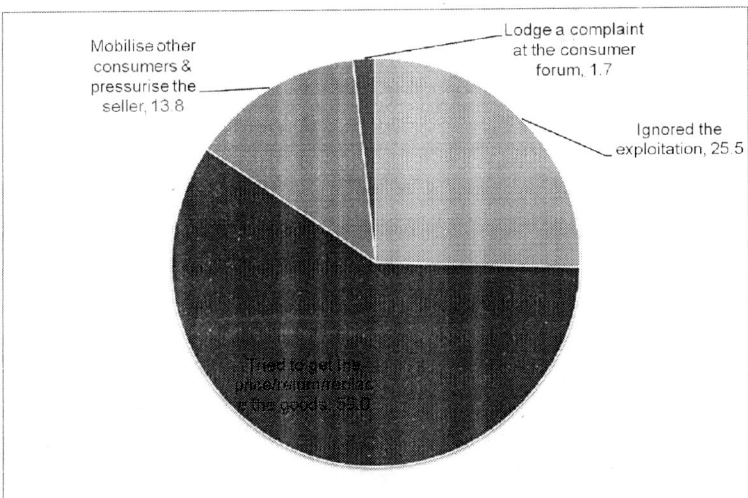

Fig. 2.5: Consumer's Action regarding Experience of Cheating

Source: CCS Field Survey.

or return or replace the goods they had purchased. 14.1 per cent of the respondents said they mobilized consumers to put pressure on the settler. Only 1.7 per cent of the respondents said that they lodged a complaint with the district forum. Large number of the respondents was not even aware about the district forum (Fig. 2.5).

Awareness about Institutional Mechanism for Consumer Protection Knowledge about Consumer Protection Act, 1986

The study also deals with the awareness about the institutional mechanism for Consumer Protection. Therefore, it was imperative to assess the level of awareness about the Consumer Protection Act, 1986 among the respondents. It is surprising that in spite of more than three decades of the existence of the Consumer Protection Act, 1986, nearly 70 per cent of the respondents are not even aware that such a legislation to protect the consumers exists in the country. Only 9.6 per cent of the respondents know about Consumer Protection Act, 1986 to a large extent while 21.1 per cent were aware about the Act to some extent only. As respondents are not aware about the Consumer Protection Act they cannot take benefit from it.

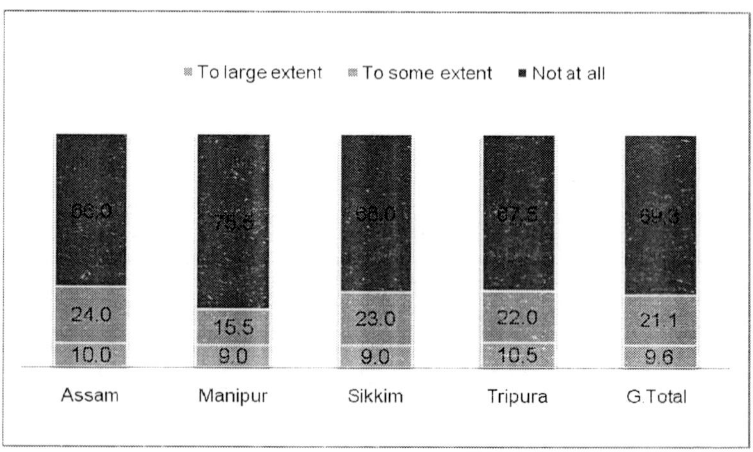

Fig. 2.6: Consumers know about Protection Consumer Protection Act, 1986

Source: CCS Field Survey.

Respondents' Knowledge as to Who is a Consumer

The Consumer Protection Act defines as to who is a consumer so that he can take the benefit of the Act to redress his complaints. 66.3 per cent of the respondents were not even aware as to who is a consumer? They replied that anyone who consumes is a consumer. Only 16.9 per cent of the respondents said that one who pays for goods or services is a consumer. 13.1 per cent said that businessmen were not consumers.

Table 2.2: Respondents Know Who is a Consumer?

States	Anyone who consumes is a consumer	One who has paid for Goods/ Services	Businessmen are not consumers	Don't know
Assam	63.7	20.3	13.6	2.4
Manipur	66.1	19.7	13.0	3.2
Sikkim	69.1	13.4	13.4	4.1
Tripura	66.3	14.3	12.2	7.1
G. Total	**66.3**	**16.9**	**13.1**	**4.2**

Source: CCS Field Survey.

Consumer Knowledge about Number of Consumer Rights under Consumer Protection Act, 1986

The Consumer Protection Act, 1986 gives six rights to consumers. However, only 29.4 per cent of the respondents answered correctly when asked as to how many rights are there under the Consumer Protection Act, 1986. 23.5 per cent of the respondents said consumers have eight rights, which 33.2 per cent said three rights and 13.9 per cent said consumers had one right.

For redressal of Consumer Complaints the 1986 Act provides for a three tier redressal mechanism at the District, State and National level. Each district has a District Forum with a pecuniary jurisdiction of Rs. 20 lakh. A consumer can file a complaint in the District Forum. However, majority of the respondents are not even aware about the existence of the district forum. 59.8 per cent of the respondents are not even aware about the district forums.

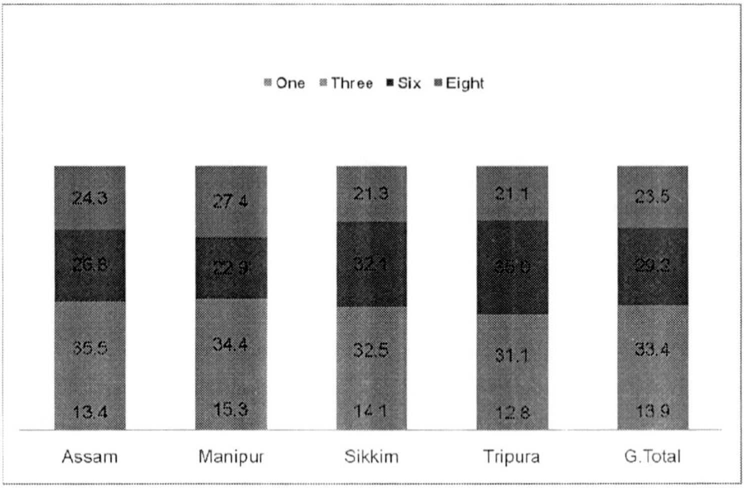

Fig. 2.7: Consumer Knowledge about the Consumer Rights under CP Act, 1986

Source: CCS Field Survey.

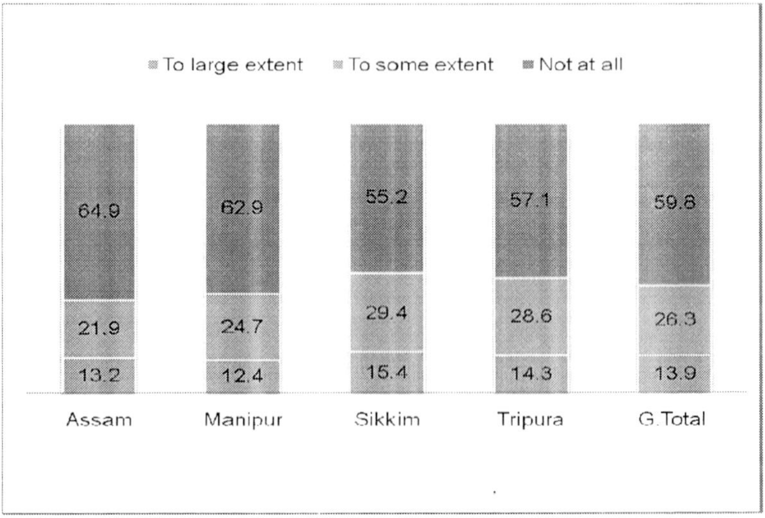

Fig. 2.8: Consumer Awareness about the Distrct Forum

Source: CCS Field Survey.

Who can file a Complaint ?

Table 2.3 reveals the responses of the respondents as to who can file a complaint in the District Forum. Accordingly 40.8 per cent of the respondents answered correctly and said that the consumer can file a complaint. 19.9 per cent said the complaint can be filed by government department, while 21.9 per cent said the complaint can be filed by the businessmen.

Table 2.3: Who can file a Complaint?

States	Consumer	Govt. Department	Businessman	Don't know
Assam	37.7	20.5	25.3	16.5
Manipur	39.9	19.2	24.7	16.2
Sikkim	44.6	19.5	18.4	17.5
Tripura	41.0	20.3	19.3	19.4
G. Total	**40.8**	**19.9**	**21.9**	**17.4**

Source: CCS Field Survey.

Have you ever filed a complaint in the District Forum ?

There are very few respondents who have filed complaint. 95.7 per cent of the respondents have never filed a complaint in the

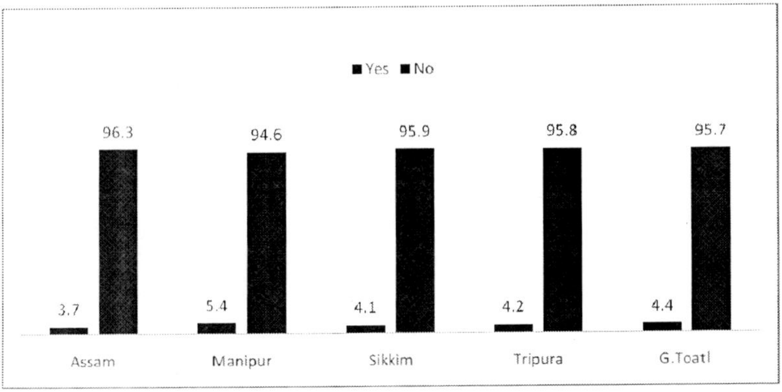

Fig. 2.9: Have Consumers ever Filed a Complaint in District Forum?
Source: CCS Field Survey.

district forum in the four sampled states. Only 4.4 per cent of the respondents said that they have filed the complaint for redressal of their grievances.

Out of these 4.4 per cent of the respondents only 10.2 per cent filed the complaint personally, 15.3 per cent took the help of NGO to file the complaint, while 74.6 per cent of the respondents filed the complaint through an advocate.

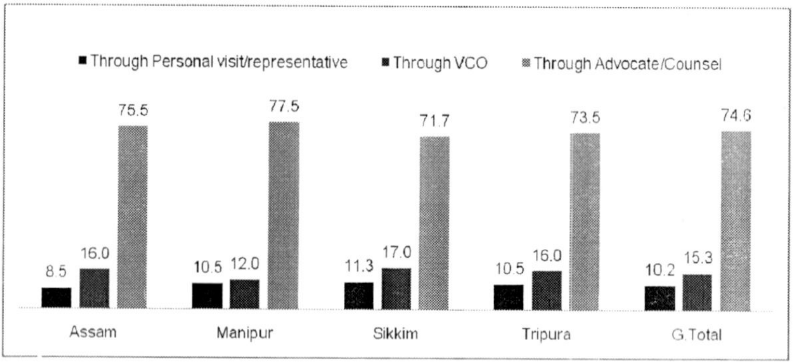

Fig. 2.10: Have Consumers ever Filed a Complaint in District Forum

Source: CCS Field Survey.

Consumer Awareness about National Consumer Helpline

National Consumer Helpline (NCH) has been set up by the Department of Consumer Affairs to help consumers seek advice, information and also file their complaints to seek redressal. The complaint can be filed through a toll free number, web, SMS, App. A Zonal Helpline of the NCH has also been set up in Guwahati to cater to NE consumers particularly in their own language. Figure 1.14 reveals that 89.5 per cent of the respondents are not even aware about the existence of NCH. Only 10.5 per cent of the respondents had approached NCH. 61.4 per cent of the respondents did not know if there was a State Consumer Helpline functioning in their state for the benefit of the consumers. Only 7.0 per cent of the respondents were aware about the functioning of the State Consumer Helpline in their States.

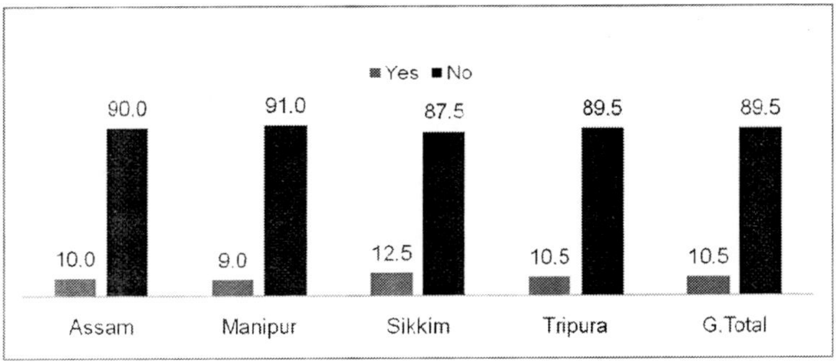

Fig. 2.11: Consumers Aware about National Consumer Helpline

Source: CCS Field Survey.

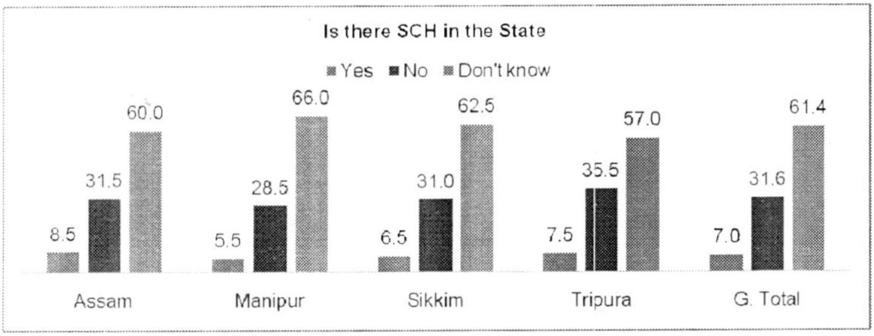

Fig. 2.12: Is there SCH in the State?

Source: CCS Field Survey.

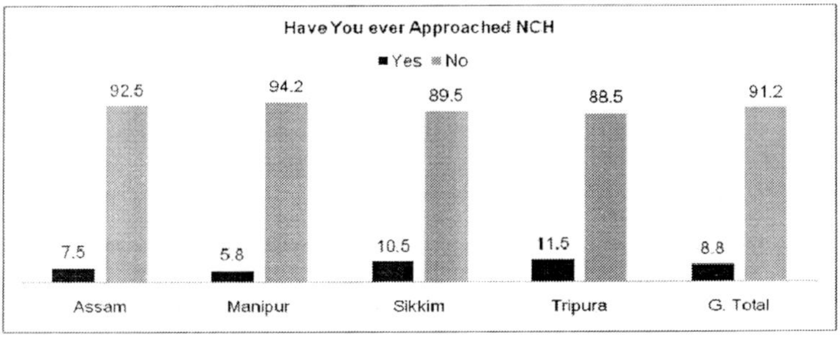

Fig. 2.13: Have You ever Approached NCH?

Source: CCS Field Survey.

Role of State Government

The respondents were asked about the role played by the State Governments in promoting consumer education and awareness. 72.1 per cent of the respondents were not aware about the State Government organizing awareness campaigns to educate consumers. Only 27.9 per cent of the respondents were aware about such programmes.

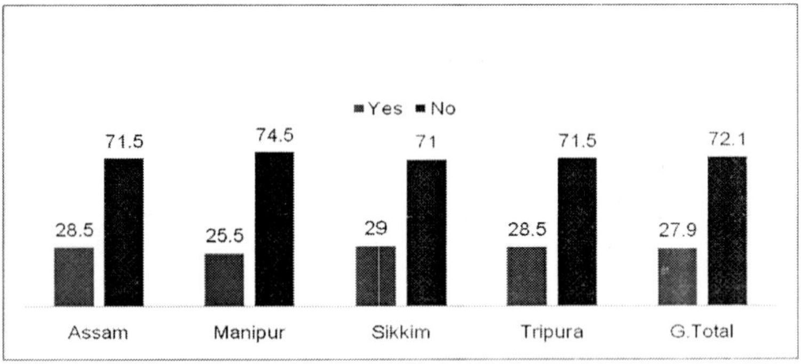

Fig. 2.14: Does State Government Otganize Consumer Awareness Campaign?

Source: CCS Field Survey.

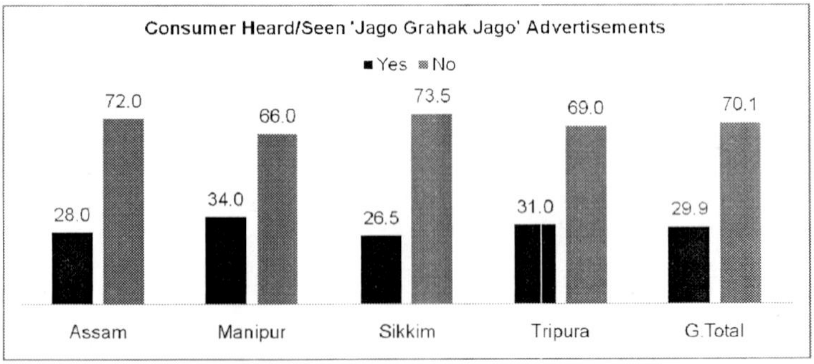

Fig. 2.15: Consumer Heared/Seen 'Jago Grahak Jago' Advertisements

Source: CCS Field Survey.

As far as the "Jago Grahak Jago" campaign of the Central Government is concerned only 29.9 per cent of the respondents had heard or seen such a campaign for the benefit of the consumers. 70.1 per cent were not even aware about such a campaign.

Observations

1. There is no awareness about consumer rights and Consumer Protection Act, 1986 in the sample states.
2. The State Governments are not serious about promoting consumer welfare in the state. No specific programmes/ schemes to educate consumers were visible in their states.
3. Most of the Consumer Affairs, Food and Public Distribution Department officials were ignorant about Consumer Welfare Fund.
4. The State Consumer Helplines are almost defunct and lack capacity and capability to help consumers.
5. The consumer movement in the states is dormant as there are few NGOs working for consumers' welfare. Those working in this area lack resources and capacity to make any meaningful impact.

Recommendations

1. There is a need to create awareness among the consumers about consumer rights, Consumer Protection Act standards, quality etc. This is very important. A professional media action plan needs to be formulated and implemented which should target various section of the society.
2. The State Government should set up Consumer Welfare Fund to promote consumer programmes and schemes in the state.
3. All stakeholders, state governments, redressal agencies, educational institutions and NGOs should work together to empower consumers.
4. Consumer clubs should be set up in schools and colleges. Consumer awareness and poster competitions should be organized at school and college level to involve school and college students in the consumer movement.

5. All computers and other accessories in the District Forums and State Commissions need to be replaced with new ones as they are all outdated. Internet speed needs to be increased.
6. Massive consumer awareness and education programmes must be organized in each state to empower consumers.
7. Media, both print and electronic media should be associated with awareness campaigns. Regular programmes must be aired. Social media should be used extensively.
8. There should be a designated Consumer Protection Officer in each state to promote and monitor consumer activities in the state.
9. Regular consumer fairs and *melas* should be organized in these states to promote consumer welfare activities.
10. Consumer education may be introduced in the school syllabus of each state at high school level.
11. Universities should be encouraged to adopt UGC module on consumer affairs and introduce it as an elective paper at under graduate level.
12. National Consumer Day and World Consumer Rights Day may be celebrated at each District Forum and State Commission. For this some financial grant should be made available.
13. Some financial grant should be given to District Forums and State Commissions for meeting day-to-day needs and also for publicity.

Conclusion

In the area of consumer education and awareness the North East Region has not been very active. The commissions are not working well. The state government has not taken steps to strengthen the consumer movement. The number of complaints being filed in the consumer commissions is very low due to lack of awareness about Consumer Rights and Responsibilities.

Notes

1. Dubey, Abhishek & Zai, Dr. Rahil Yusuf (2010). *North-East India: An Untapped Emerging Market*, Munich, GRIN Verlag, https://www.grin.com/document/150051, accessed 31-12-2019.
2. Hazarika, Bhabesh (2015). *An Insight to the Structure of the North East Indian Retail Sector*, Munich Personal RePEc Archive, at https://mpra.ub.uni-muenchen.de/63987/ MPRA Paper No.63987, posted01May201505:41UTC
3. FICCI-KPMG,(2016). *Leveraging the Digital Connect: North Eastern India*, https://ficci.in/spdocument/20775/FICCI-KPMG-DigitalConnect-NE-India.pdf
4. Suneera Tandon, *Upscale brands train sights on the north-east,* Updated: 18 February 2013, 11:24 PM IST, https://www.livemint.com/Industry/dntuQ6Oy08U7magzR5lPvJ/Upscale-brands-train- sights-on-the-northeast.html

3

Behaviour of College Students on Use of Cell Phone in Nagaland

A Case Study

Gopal Chetri and *Ratan Kaurinta*

Introduction

Mobile phone has become a necessity for every human being. One cannot imagine the life without cell phone. Cell phone has entirely changed the way people connect. Today one can call, send out text, read emails, play video games as well as read and modify documents on the move. The cell phone has actually ended up being part and parcel of individuals' lives.

It is a devise which comes with super impressive features related to entertainment and enjoyment. It is also useful in studies and managing the business affairs. Smartphone with internet facility is a portable computer system, which is convenient to use. It is like holding the entire globe in our palm. In fact, it is the most amazing invention of the age. Despite its high-tech functions advantages and increasing popularity, the smartphone has negatively influenced the behaviour of individuals and society as a whole. Parents want to give all the facilities to their children at a tender age to help them carve a perfect career path. Youngsters insist that their parents purchase the most expensive and latest Smartphone, which in itself is the origin of all the problems apparently. Students generally have peer pressure to maintain their relationship and image, that's why they want to own the most fashionable gadget of the era—the Smartphone. Without Smartphone, students feel isolated from their friends' circle and harbour fear of missing out (FOMO). Students are stressed trying to maintain a proper communication level with their friends and keep themselves updated with the latest version of apps available for gaming, social networking, entertainments etc.

Now-a-days students' spend most of their time listening to music, playing mobile games, chatting and calling friends, following social media and are lost in the virtual world of entertainment and fun. Smartphone that has been developed to solve the problems of human being, itself has turned into a cause of problems for many of the youngsters. Anxiety, stress and depression are some of the problems faced by students due to 24-hour connectivity with friends and social media. According to a study, students fail to set goals for themselves due a confused state of mind. What leads to a confused state of mind? Teenagers get deep into a delirious state of mind due to their continuous engagement with their phone all the time. They do not sleep well, constantly check their phone, mind remains pre-occupied and are full of stress. It increases aggression in students, loss of self-confidence and leads to a disastrous life, which becomes burden to family, society and country as a whole.

In short, excessive use of mobile phones is becoming a distraction for students and is wasting their time. They remain immersed into the virtual world to an extent that they forget all other important activities.

Statement of the Problem

Being a part of today's technological world, growing use of mobile phones and other gadgets is considerably harming the younger generation. Students are developing a strong connection with their mobile phones, which is leading to a massive loss in their concentration and time spent on studies. Parents and teachers usually face problem in combating the distraction of students. Anything which is available, accessible, new, fast and related to information and technology tends to attract a lot of people. When children see their parents, family members and everybody in their surroundings using cell phones, they adapt this as a natural phenomenon. One of the negative effects on students is—they are getting addicted to mobile phones. They play games, chat, and talk to their friends on their mobile phones most of the times. This is the reason why they do not get time for studies. In fact, students are more interested in wasting their time on mobile phones, rather than spending it on their studies.

Students have the right to receive the transformational and appreciating value from the education system, and equal right to understand what that value is and how well it is delivering. Students have to understand the value that comes from learning and teaching. However, the disturbing fact is that most of the present generation is bogged down with their cell phone wherever they go. Human touch and feeling is missing within their family, friends and people around them. If the menace of using excessive phone by the students' is not stopped, huge generation gap will arise in the near future. Availability of free internet data service and attractive offers by the service providers further entice the students to remain busy with their cell phone rather than concentrating on their studies and doing other activities. Therefore, parents, teachers and other stakeholders should take positive steps to curb this excessive use of cell phones through a mechanism that will divert the attention of the students towards achieving their goal rather than wasting their valuable time with cell phone, which will do no good to them.

Significance of the Study

It is the prayer and desire of all the parents to see their children grow and achieve success. The young generation of today has lost the track because of the phenomenon created by technology as it has diverted the attention of the students from their studies. Parents and colleges administration are confused and severely affected because of the advent of sophisticated gadgets and attractive services provided by the network operators. It has become difficult to combat the menace of smart phone.

So far, no research has been conducted in Nagaland in respect of use of cell phone and its consequences in the life of younger generation. The research study was, therefore, conducted to devise a mechanism that will help the students to utilize their time judiciously in their studies and at the same time remain in touch with the modern gadgets. This study also looked at the impact of reducing the use of cell phone on the life of students and their academic performance.

Review of Literature

Some researches as well as general studies have conducted over the year relating to the use of cell phone. However, no study has been carried out so far pertaining to the use of cell phones by college students in Nagaland. An effort to review some of the important works having a bearing on the present study has been made.

According to a report published in the *Guardian*, a research done by Louis-Philippe Boland and Richard Murphy, published by the Centre for Economic Performance at the London School of Economics on "Communication: The Impact of Mobile Phones on Student Performance" found that after schools banned mobile phones, the test scores of students aged 16 improved by 6.4 per cent. The economists reckon that this is the "equivalent of adding five days to the school year".

According to report published in the *Daily Mail*, a new study claims that heavy internet and mobile phone users are prone to lack of concentration and forget things easily. This also affects their awareness and eventually leads to passive mind. Moreover, this also leads to weak focus and attention.

The World Health Organization (WHO) classifies cell phone radiation as a "possible human carcinogen" due to an increased risk of brain cancer from long-term and heavy use of cell phones.

The Netherlands' study is not the first one to show an EEG change because of acute exposure to cell phone radiation. There are three main reasons why people are concerned that cell phones (also known as "mobile" or "wireless" telephones) might have the potential to cause certain types of cancer or other health problems: Cell phones emit radio frequency energy (radio waves), a form of non-ionizing radiation, from their antennas.

Researchers at the University of Nebraska-Lincoln found that university students check their phones approximately 11 times a day while in class. More than 80 per cent have stated that this affect their learning and a quarter admitted that their grades had fallen as a result.

According to a 2011 survey by the U.K. communications regulator Ofcom, 51 per cent of adults and 65 per cent of teenagers said they have used their smart phone while socializing with others. This proves that even when people are having face-to-face communication, the phone constantly distracts them.

Objectives of the Study

The key objectives of the study are to:

1. examine the consumer behaviour on use of cell phone amongst the college students;
2. compare the behaviour of male and female students on use of cell phone; and
3. suggest the best use of smart phone and technology amongst the students community.

Methodology

The case study is based on empirical approach. In order to achieve the objectives, information was collected from both primary and secondary sources. The secondary information was collected mainly from internet.

The primary data were collected from 100 college students through convenience random sampling method from the district of Kohima, Nagaland using structured questionnaires. Data so collected was analyzed and interpreted theoretically, to draw the inferences and conclusions.

Sample Design

The population of the study comprised College students from the district of Kohima, Nagaland. Convenience sampling method was used to collect the data. The target population of this study consisted of 100 college students (fifty males and fifty females) randomly drawn from the universe of Kohima District of Nagaland.

Tools of Data Collection

A well-designed structured questionnaire was used for collecting primary data from the sample students. The questionnaire consisted of two parts:

1. First part of questionnaire contained information of respondents regarding personal and cell phone details.
2. The second part of the questionnaire had questions regarding use of cell phones.

Statistical Techniques Applied

The data collected using structured questionnaire was classified and tabulated. Statistical tools, such as Mean, Percentage, Graphs and Diagrams, were used to find out the relevance and to interpret the collected data to draw meaningful conclusions.

Analysis and Interpretation

The analysis and interpretation of data so collected from the primary sources is given below:

Table 3.1: Sample Respondents according to Gender

Gender	Frequency	Percentage
Male	50	50
Female	50	50
Total	**100**	**100**

Source: Primary Data.

The primary data consisted of 50 male and 50 female college students selected through convenient sampling method from the district of Kohima.

Table 3.2: Social Status of Respondents

Social status	Frequency			Percentage		
	Male	Female	Total	Male	Female	Average
ST	35	41	76	70	82	76
SC	7	1	8	14	2	8
OBC	3	1	4	6	2	4
General	5	7	12	10	14	12
Total	**50**	**50**	**100**	**100**	**100**	**100**

Source: Primary Data.

Table 3.2 indicates that the highest numbers of student respondents were Scheduled Tribe, which comprised 76 per cent of the total population. Only 24 per cent are SC, OBC and General category. Majority of the sample respondents belong to Scheduled Tribe.

Table 3.3: Parental Income of Sample Respondents

Income of parents (in Rupees)	Frequency			Percentage		
	Male	Female	Total	Male	Female	Average
Less than 20,000	20	23	43	40	46	43
20001 to 40000	21	18	39	42	36	39
40001 to 60000	6	7	13	12	14	13
60001 and above	3	2	5	6	4	5
Total	**50**	**50**	**100**	**100**	**100**	**100**

Source: Primary Data.

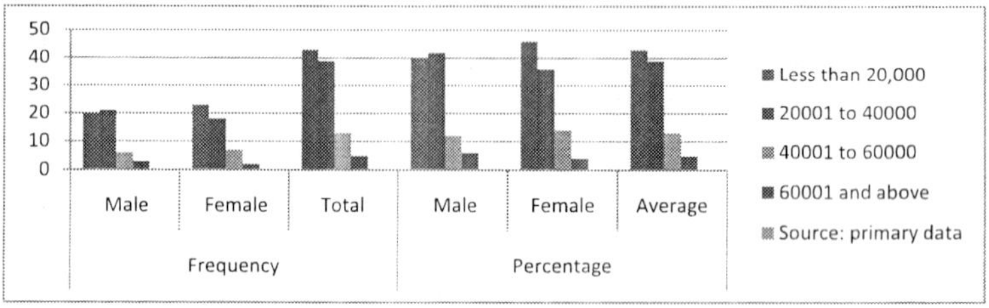

Fig. 3.1: Income of the Respondents' Parents

From Table 3.3 and Fig. 3.1, it is concluded that income of 82 per cent of the respondents' parents is less than Rupees 40,000 per month. In only 18 per cent of the respondents, parents' income is above Rupees 40,000 per month.

Table 3.4: Brand of cell phone used by Respondents

Brand of cell phone	Frequency			Percentage		
	Male	Female	Total	Male	Female	Average
Micromax	10	14	24	20	28	24
Samsung	7	5	12	14	10	12
Gionee	3	3	6	6	6	6
Vivo	5	2	7	10	4	7
Intex	5	6	11	10	12	11
Panasonic	1	1	2	2	2	2
Oppo	3	2	5	6	4	5
Nokia	2	0	2	4	0	2
Lyf	2	2	4	4	4	4
Lava	3	3	6	6	6	6
iphone	2	5	7	4	10	7
Others	6	7	13	12	14	13
Not in use	1	0	0	2	0	1
Total	**50**	**50**	**100**	**100**	**100**	**100**

Source: Primary Data.

Table 3.4 given above represents that the respondent students use different brands of cell phones. The maximum number of respondents, comprising 24 per cent, use Micromax brand. It can thus be concluded that there is no particular choice of brand of cell phone being used by the respondent students.

Table 3.5 describes that the most used network service in Nagaland is Airtel followed by Vodaphone and Jio which comprise 33 per cent, 30 per cent and 24 per cent respectively. Only 1 per cent of the respondents use BSNL. It has been found that 99 per cent of the college students have access to internet network services.

Table 3.5: Network Services in Use

Network service provider	Frequency			Percentage		
	Male	Female	Total	Male	Female	Average
Airtel	15	18	33	30	36	33
Jio	17	7	24	34	14	24
Vodaphone	14	16	30	28	32	30
BSNL	0	1	1	0	2	1
Idea	4	7	11	8	14	11
Aircel	5	6	11	10	12	11
Not in use	1	0	1	2	0	1
Other	0	0	0	0	0	0

Source: Primary Data.

It is thus concluded that the major network players in Nagaland are Airtel, Vodaphone and Jio. Almost all of the students use cell phones and have access to internet.

Table 3.6: Generation of Internet Data in Use

Generation	Frequency			Percentage		
	Male	Female	Total	Male	Female	Average
2G	0	3	3	0	6	3
3G	21	30	51	42	60	51
4G	28	17	45	56	34	45
None	1	0	1	2	0	1
Total	**50**	**50**	**100**	**100**	**100**	**100**

Source: Primary Data.

Table 3.6 reflects that 51 per cent (in average) of the respondents have access to 3G service closely followed by 4G service that comprises 45 per cent. Majority of the female respondents have access to 3G service, whereas, majority of the male respondents use 4G internet service in Nagaland.

Table 3.7: Purpose of Using Cell Phone

Purpose	Frequency			Percentage		
	Male	Female	Total	Male	Female	Average
To remain connected	39	37	76	78	74	76
Social networking	38	38	76	76	76	76
Gaming	24	8	32	48	16	32
Entertainment	23	9	32	46	18	32
Others	13	4	17	26	08	17

Source: Primary Data.

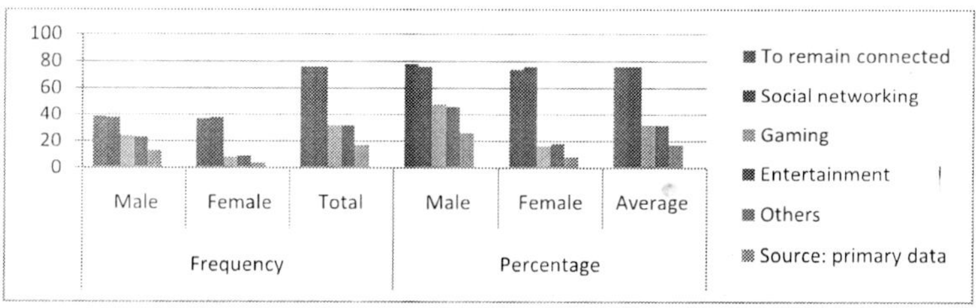

Fig. 3.2: Purpose for Use of Cell Phone by Students

Table 3.7 and Fig. 3.2, depict that out of 50 male respondents, 39 use cell phones to remain connected with their family and friends, 38 of them remain busy with social networking, 24 of them use it for gaming and 23 of them for entertainment. Hence, majority of the male respondents use cell phone to remain in the virtual world. It was found that the purpose of use of the cell phones for female respondents was the same as that of male.

The study also shows that 48 per cent of male respondents play game on their smart phone, whereas only 16 per cent of the female respondents play game. It has also found that 46 per cent of the male entertain themselves through the cell phones and 18 per cent of the female respondents use it for entertainment purpose.

It has been concluded that majority of the students use cell phone to remain connected, for social networking, gaming and entertainment purpose. Few respondents use phones for other beneficial purposes.

Table 3.8: Time Spent on Cell Phone

Time spent (in hours)	Frequency			Percentage		
	Male	Female	Total	Male	Female	Average
Less than one hour	4	0	4	8	0	4
1 to 2 hours	13	16	29	26	32	29
2 to 3 hours	13	13	26	26	26	26
More than 3 hours	20	21	41	40	42	41
Total	**50**	**50**	**100**	**100**	**100**	**100**

Source: Primary Data.

The information depicted in Table 3.8 shows that 41 per cent of the respondents spent more than three hours of their time on cell phones and 55 per cent of them spent one to three hours everyday on the cell phone. Only 4 per cent of the sample respondents use cell phone for less than one hour everyday. It is thus concluded that about 96 per cent of college students in Nagaland use cell phone for more than one hour everyday. There is no sinificant difference in time spent by male and female students of Nagaland.

Table 3.9: Source for Recharge of Data Packages and Top Up

Money obtained	Frequency			Percentage		
	Male	Female	Total	Male	Female	Average
Parent	37	43	80	74	86	80
Relatives	1	0	1	2	0	1
Friends	0	0	0	0	0	0
Others	12	7	19	24	14	19
Total	**50**	**50**	**100**	**100**	**100**	**100**

Source: Primary Data.

Table 3.9 depicts that 80 per cent of the respondent students recharge their cell phone or put top-up by obtaining money from their parents. Hence, parents are the main source of supplying money to students for the recharge of their cell phones.

Table 3.10: Time Invested in Studies by Respondents

Time spent in studies	Frequency			Percentage		
	Male	Female	Total	Male	Female	Average
Less than one hour	17	12	29	34	24	29
1 to 2 hours	26	23	49	52	46	49
2 to 3 hours	5	7	12	10	14	12
3 hours and more	2	8	10	4	16	10
Total	**50**	**50**	**100**	**100**	**100**	**100**

Source: Primary Data.

The above table highlights that on an average 29 per cent of the sample respondents spent less than one hour in their studies, and 49 per cent—about one to two hours. Time of two to three hours for studies is devoted by 12 per cent and more than three hours by 10 per cent only. Out of ten respondents spending more than three hours on their studies, 80 per cent are females. It has concluded that majority of college students in Nagaland spent less time on their studies.

Table 3.11: Respondents Keeping Cell Phone 'On' During Study Hour

Keeping cell on	Frequency			Percentage		
	Male	Female	Total	Male	Female	Average
Always	6	12	18	12	24	18
Sometime	32	25	57	64	50	57
Never	12	13	25	24	26	25
Total	**50**	**50**	**100**	**100**	**100**	**100**

Source: Primary Data.

Table 3.11 and Fig. 3.3 given above, depict that 24 per cent of female respondents and 12 per cent of male respondents always kept their cell phone on during study hours. Whereas, 24 per cent of male and 26 per cent of female respondents always kept their cell phone off during study hour. It is thus concluded that majority of the respondent students, kept their cell phone on during study hour.

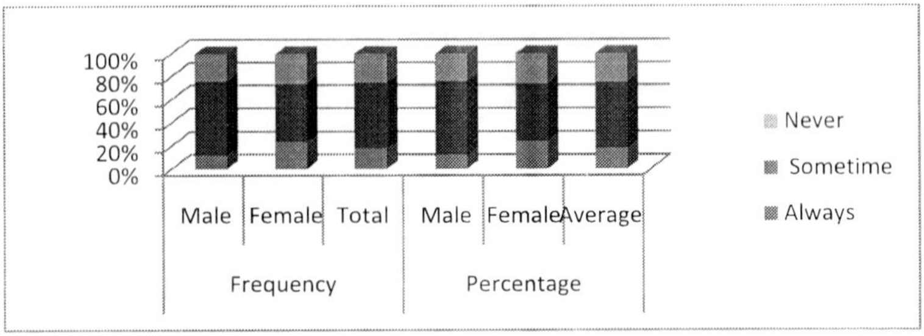

Fig. 3.3: Respondents Keeping Cell Phone on during Study Hours

Table 3.12: Respondents' Views about Cell Phone during Study Hour

Internet service	Frequency			Percentage		
	Male	Female	Total	Male	Female	Average
Helpful when on	21	12	33	42	24	33
Helpful when off	9	13	22	18	26	22
Disturbing	6	11	17	12	22	17
Divert attention	14	14	28	28	28	28
Total	**50**	**50**	**100**	**100**	**100**	**100**

Source: Primary Data.

Table 3.12 shows that 42 per cent of the male respondents stated that keeping cell phone on during study hour is helpful. Whereas, 18 per cent said keeping cell off is helpful. 12 per cent were of the view that it is disturbing and 28 per cent commented that keeping phone on during study hour diverts attention and concentration. On the other hand, 24 per cent female respondents were of the view that it is helpful when it is on, 26 per cent said it is helpful when it is off, for 22 per cent it is disturbing and for 28 per cent it diverts attention and concentration.

Major Findings

The following findings have been drawn from the study:

1. The finding from primary data of the study shows that majority of the college students in Nagaland belong to Scheduled Tribe. Students belonging to Scheduled Caste, Other Backward tribes and general are less than 25 per cent of the total students.
2. Parental income of around 43 per cent of the students in Nagaland is less than Rs. 20,000 per month and of 39 per cent it is between Rs. 20,000 to Rs. 40,000. Thus, majority of the students' parental income is less than Rupees forty thousand per month.
3. Regarding the choice of brand of cell phones, it has been found that there is no particular preference amongst the students. The study reveals that the respondents use different brand of cell phones to fulfil their purposes.
4. The most used network service in Nagaland by the students is Airtel closely followed by Vodaphone and Jio. Students do not prefer much of the other network service provider like Aircel and Idea. Only 1 per cent of the students use data service provided by BSNL.
5. Majority of the students' in Nagaland use 3G service closely followed by 4G.
6. It is found that out of 50 male respondents, 78 per cent of them use cell phone to remain connected with their family and friends, and 76 per cent remain busy with social networking, 48 per cent gaming and 46 per cent in entertainment. Hence, majority of the male respondents use cell phone to remain in the virtual world. Comparatively, female respondents also use the cell phones for the same purpose as that of male. The study also reveals that more male students play game in their smart phones than that of female students. It is also found that female students spent less time in entertainment than that of male students.

7. 41 per cent of the students (average of male and female) in Nagaland spent more than three hours of their time in cell phones and 55 per cent of them spent one to three hours everyday in the cell phone. Only 4 per cent of the students' use cell phone for less than one hour everyday.
8. Almost all of the college students in Nagaland use cell phone for hours everyday. There is no significant difference in time spent by male and female students on the cell phone.
9. Majority of the students get money from their parents to recharge or put top up in their cell phone.
10. Majority of the college students in Nagaland do not invest sufficient time on studies. Female students study more than male sudents.
11. 24 per cent female and 12 per cent male respondents always keep their cell phone on during study hours. Whereas, 24 per cent of male and 26 per cent of female respondents always keep their cell phone off during study hour. Majority of the students' in Nagaland keep their cell phone on during study hours.
12. 42 per cent of the male respondents stated that keeping 'cell phone on' during study hour is helpful. Whereas, 18 per cent said it is helpful when 'cell is off'. 12 per cent it is disturbing and 28 per cent commented that keeping phone on during study hour diverts attention and concentration. On the other hand, for 24 per cent of the female respondents' it is helpful when it is on, 26 per cent helpful when it is off, for 22 per cent it is disturbing and for 28 per cent it diverts attention and concentration.

Suggestions

The following suggestions will help the students and youngsters largely for the gainful use of cell phone and derive benefits out of it rather than wasting their valuable time engaging in the activities that will not do any good to them:

1. To use the cell phone for necessities only, viz. important calls and messages, downloading the study materials, e-commerce and other unavoidable and useful purpose.
2. To avoid social networking, gaming and entertainment as far as possible.
3. To observe no cell phone day, once in a week by all the students.
4. To switch off the cell phone during study hours and keep aside to avoid the temptation.
5. Colleges and schools authorities are strongly recommended to ban the students from bringing the cell phone in the campus.
6. Parents should know the purpose of their children regarding the use of cell phone. They need to remain vigil and should not allow them to use during study hour.
7. Law enforcing agency should look into the matter related to attractive offer provided by service operator. As the motive of the operator is to attract their customer and let them keep busy with the service provided by them. Social sites which do not suit the youngsters should be restricted or even banned.
8. To educate the students about the best use of cell phone in schools and colleges.

Conclusion

It has been concluded from the studies that majority of the college students in Nagaland belongs to Scheduled Tribe. Most of the students' parental income is less than Rupees forty thousand per month. Ninety nine per cent of the college students use cell phone in Nagaland.

Regarding the brand of cell phones, there is no particular preference amongst the students. Airtel followed by Vodaphone and Jio are the most preferred network service used by the students in Nagaland. Only one per cent of the students use BSNL service. Majority of the students use 3G service closely followed by 4G.

Most of the male and female students use cell phone for more than three hours everyday to remain connected, social networking, gaming and entertainment. Hence, majority of the students remain busy with cell phone in the virtual world. Parents are the main source of finance to purchase top up and to recharge the cell phone balance.

Majority of the students in Nagaland waste valuable time entertaining themselves or visiting social sites through smart phone and invest less time in their studies. Comparatively, female students invest more time than male in the studies. Hence, female students are performing better than male. Majority of the students in Nagaland keep their cell phone 'on' during study hour and get distracted.

"Smart phones were invented to 'solve the human problems' but in contrast, it has become a big problem for the students and youngsters because of its misuse'. Many of the students' performance have gone down after purchasing the smart phone. Parents and teachers are undergoing tough time dealing with their children and students regarding the use of cell phone, as they are lost in the virtual world."

References

Arshi (January 6, 2017). *7 Harmful Side Effects of Mobile Phones on Teenagers,* retrieved from http://www.momjunction.com/articles/side-effects-of-mobile-phones-on-teenagers_00352682/#gref

Berry, Kristen. (August 13, 2015). *How Do Cell Phones Negatively Affect the Health of Teens?* retrieved from www.livestrong.com,Parenting.

CBS News (May 20, 2014). "What do mobile phones do to teenage brains?" *CBS News,* retrieved from https://www.cbsnews.com/news/what-do-mobile-phones-do-to-teenage-brains/

Murtaza, Khuram. (December 19, 2012). Negative Effects of Cell Phones on Youth, retrieved from https://www.siasat.pk/forum/showthread.php?151984-Negative-Effects-of-Cell-Phones-on-Youth

Ravidchandran, S.V. (2009). *Positive and Negative Effects of Mobile Phones for Teenagers,* retrieved from https://brightkite.com/essay-on/positive-and-negative-effects-of-mobile-phones-for-teenagers

Reed, M. (November 15, 2011). "The Influence of Mobile Phones on Teenagers", *Australian Science*, retrieved from http://www.australianscience.com.au/.../the-influence-of-mobile-phones-on-teenagers/

The Phone Town News, Positive and Negative Effects of Mobile Phones, retrieved from http://www.thephonetown.com/positive-and-negative-effects-of-mobile-phones/

4

Customer Satisfaction Pertaining to the Banks of Manipur

N. Tejmani Singh and *P. Chinglen Singh*

Introduction

The business of banking is as old as the civilization itself. As early as 2,000 B.C., the Babylonians used their temples for lending at higher rates of interest against gold and silver which had been left with them for safe detention. In ancient times, the main functions of the banks related to granting of loans to individuals or the state in times of crisis. Banking institutions during pre-Independence period primarily consisted of indigenous banks, *sahukars, nidhis*, loan offices etc. In 1850, the passing of the Joint Stock Company Act greatly helped in establishment of many commercial banks. Later on in 1921, the Imperial Bank of India (now known as State Bank of India) and in 1935 RBI was also established. Banking business has since evolved manifold to current techno savvy form.

Banks these days provide a variety of services ranging from opening a saving account to interest banking, granting loans to selling insurance, and providing locker facilities to transferring money abroad. Their customers come from all classes of society from a salaried group to a Multi-National Corporation having its business activities all around the world. The banks have to convince all the customers belonging to diverse social groups. Banking has, therefore, become more multifaceted and requires specialized skills.

In this background, a study on bank's observation in the mind of customers and comparative analysis of services of private and public sector banks sounds interesting. Such analysis will provide the banks with a quantitative and qualitative approximate of their services as perceived by their customers.

Geiger (1975) carried out study to set up the needs of customers. Social position of the bank's customers and the perceptions that the customers had of banks were studied along with customers decision of the range of services that the banks had to offer, the effectiveness of various advertising and other sales promoting measures, and the customers' will to save. Findings indicated that satisfied customers are more optimistic in nature than those who are critical of what their banks have to offer them. The study by Syed Asad Akbar (1990) highlights the need for a more customer oriented approach to bank marketing with more emphasis on improved marketing strategies. Stressing on the need for a 'plan oriented marketing', suggestions were made that new product development should be done on a continuing basis and schemes which have failed to take off should be reviewed and necessary decision should be taken if same are to modified or dropped. Lewis and Birminghan (1991) studied the needs, attitudes and behaviour of youth market for financial services and found that the youth market is not homogenous in terms of needs. Boyd *et al.* (1994) conducted a study on consumer choice criteria in financial institution selection in USA and found that reputations and interest rates of loans as well as savings rates are more important than friendliness of employees, modern facilities and drive-in-services. On the other hand, Rajagopla Nair (1994) in his study on rural bank marketing found that safety and liquidity are the major prerequisites for deposits by rural customers and that the interest rate on fixed and demand deposits is not at all a decisive factor for rural bank depositors to deposit their savings with commercial banks.

Huu Phuong Ta and Kar Yin Har (2000) studied bank selection preferences of undergraduates in Singapore. In the study, nine criteria for selecting bank and five banks were identified, and the decision problem was structured into a three-level hierarchy using the analytic hierarchy process. The result indicated that undergraduates emphasize more on the pricing and product dimensions of bank services.

Hallowell Roger (1996) studied customer satisfaction in banks and found banks should target and serve only those customers whose needs it can meet better than its competitors in a profitable manner. By adopting this strategy customers will be retained for longer periods, use multiple products; recommend the bank to their friends and relations who may be the source of superior returns to the bank's shareholders.

As per Meidan (1976), about 90 per cent of the respondents banked at the branch adjacent to their home place and place of work. Convenience, in terms of location, was found to be the single most important factor for selecting a bank.

Dutta *et al.* (2009), conducted a study to investigate perception of expectations of customers across all the banks in India. It was found that foreign banks were the most preferred banks followed by private banks and public banks.

Literature Review

Comparison of services by banks is under active and extensive discussion among academicians and bank personnel. Survey and research have been conducted both by academic researchers and practitioners on the various aspects of services by banks in particular both in Centre as well as State.

Smith (1990) studied the four unique characteristics of services —intangibility, inseparability, heterogeneity and perishability and how it effects clients' perceptions of quality service from banks. The study exposed that intensifying competition and increasing customer expectations have created a climate where quality is considered to be a major strategic variable for improving customer satisfactions and thereby contributing to the profitability of financial service providers.

According to Liang *et al.* (2004), the service quality attributes are of two types; one is product related, and the other one non-product related. These attributes may generate the perceptions of symbolic, functional or experiential benefits among customers. The study results strongly highlighted the fact that customer satisfaction positively affects customer's belief and commitment on service provider, which in turn affects customer's behavioural loyalty.

Sarin and Anil (2009) recommended that manpower in service organizations must work with the focal point of satisfying the customer. Banking should bring out the areas requiring upgrading and further throws light on the measures that customers feel should be adopted in order to improve the quality of services. According to Laroche and Manning (1986), Location convenience, speed of service, competence and friendliness of bank personnel scored most of the points with maximum value in banking services.

Aurara and Malhotra (1997) studied the level of customer satisfaction and some marketing strategies in both private and public sector banks in India. They have found six factors of customer satisfaction in public sector banks, viz. routine operations, price, situational, environmental, technology, and interactive. But in private sector banks, they found seven factors in total, having staff factor as the first ranked and situational factor as the lowest ranked items. Instead of price factor, promotional factors have been explored by researchers in private sector banks. As compared to public sector, private sector bank customers' level of satisfaction is comparatively more. Proper training and development of bank staff, regular market survey, personalizing the service, efforts to avoid long queues in bank, and attractive environment are the key optional strategies in public sector bank.

Objectives of the Study

1. To examine the outlook and the level of satisfaction of the customers towards the services rendered by public and private sector banks.

2. To study the preferences and priorities towards types of services offered by the public and private sector banks.

Limitations of the Study

There are certain limitations. These are discussed as follows:

1. The researcher believes that the result of this study may be limited in terms of generalization because it refers only to a single city and so cannot be held true for the other areas of country.
2. The sample of the study consisted of only160 respondents due to time constraints.
3. The questionnaires were mostly filled by the customers in the presence of bank officials, so it is quite likely that the respondents may avoid giving negative responses fearing retaliation.

Research Hypothesis

Ho: There is no difference in satisfactions level of customer in public and private banks.

HA: Only some of the selected attributes of customer satisfaction are correlated.

Methodology and Research Design

The methodology and design adopted for the study was as follows.

Area of study: The study has been conducted in Imphal city.

Period of the study: The present research study is related to "Consumer satisfaction pertaining to the banks of Manipur".

Data collection: This study is based on questionnaire method. Primary data were collected from men and women respondents living in Imphal city. People from all walks of life were contacted. The total number of respondents was 160.

The researchers have enclosed customers from six banks, three each from public sector and private sector. Under public sector bank State Bank of India, Punjab National Bank and Oriental Bank of Commerce were selected and ICICI, HDFC and Axis Bank were selected among private sector banks.

Sampling: A sample of 160 customers has been selected using convenient sampling method. The data had been interpreted satisfactorily whenever and wherever needed.

Analysis and Findings of the Study

Reliability Analysis

In this study reliability was examined on all items. As a test of reliability Cronbach's Alpha was adopted to signify internal consistency. Table 4.1, shows the reliability test with all values greater than threshold of 0.60 (Walsh, 1995). Hence it can be concluded that the items reliably determine the defined constructs.

Table 4.1: Results of Reliability Test

Variables	Cronbach alpha
Services by teller	0.67
Relation with manager	0.89
Branch facility	0.80
Loan services	0.83
Telephone enquiry	0.67

Source: Personal calculation using SPSS.

Comparison between Public and Private Sector Banks Showing the Consequence of Banking Services on Customer Satisfaction

As the descriptive statistics in Table 4.2 highlights a significant difference between public and private banks in all the variables, it was determined to examine whether the differences are significant or not. For this purpose independent sample t-test was performed. This test is used when there are two experimental conditions and different subjects were assigned to each condition. Table 4.2 shows there is significant relationship between all the variables and the ownership of bank. Table 4.2 shows that private sector banks are as long as better services to customer in terms of services provided by teller as well as relationship with managers. It also shows that private sector banks are providing better infrastructure amenities as compared to public sector banks. Table 4.2 shows that customer satisfaction is higher in private banks than in public banks. Table 4.2 also infers that customer satisfaction is largely dependent upon their relationship with senior staff and managers of the bank.

Table 4.2: Independent Sample t-test showing the effect of banking services on customer satisfaction

Variables	Mean		Standard Deviation		t-value
	Public sector	Private sector	Public sector	Private sector	
Services by teller	11.075	11.635	2.89	3.51	2.20**
Relation with manager	13.435	13.785	4.69	4.55	0.958**
Branch facility	10.575	11.35	4.02	4.75	2.224**
Loan services	13.835	13.20	2.29	4.57	-2.23
Telephone enquiry	7.075	7.425	2.89	3.05	1.486**

**Significance at 0.01 level. *Significance at 0.05 levels.

Source: Personal calculation using SPSS.

Correlation among Attributes Selected for Measuring Customer Satisfaction

Table 4.3 shows correlation of attributes, viz. services offered by teller, rapport with manager, branch facilities, loan facilities and enquiry on telephone for measuring customer satisfaction. Table 4.3 shows that all the attributes are correlated.

Table 4.3: Correlation of attributes selected for measuring customer satisfaction

Attributes	Services by teller	Services by manager	Branch facility	Loan services	Telephone enquiry
Services by teller	1				
Relation with manager	0.759**	1			

(*Contd.*)

Branch facility	0.699**	0.799**	1		
Loan services	0.192*	0.24**	0.287**	1	
Telephone enquiry	0.37**	0.525**	0.541**	0.256**	1

*Correlation significant at 0.05.
**Correlation significant at 0.01 levels.
Source: Personal calculation using SPSS.

Regression

Table 4.4 shows multiple correlations between branch facilities and services by teller (0.699), relation with manager (0.799) and telephone enquiry (0.541). This Table shows that branch facility is positively correlated with teller services, relationship with manager, and telephone enquiry thus contributing to customer satisfaction.

Table 4.4: Linear Regression of Attributes selected for measuring customer satisfaction

Variables	**R**	**R square**	**Adjusted R square**	**Standardized co-efficient Beta**	**T-value**	**Sign**
Services by teller	0.699	0.488	0.485	0.195	2.767	0.006**
Relation with manager	0.799	0.639	0.636	0.476	5.149	0.000**
Loan services	0.287	0.082	0.076	0.008	0.164	0.870
Telephone enquiry	0.541	0.293	0.289	0.154	2.925	0.004**

*Correlation significant at 0.05 levels.
**Correlation significant at 0.01 levels.
Source: Personal calculation using SPSS.

Discussion and Conclusion

The length of time that a customer spends with his relationship officer or manager is very important. As per the recent data 68 per cent of the customers have been with their respective relationship officer/manager for more than 2 years. The relationship marketing should be emphasized upon and special training should be provided to all the corporate staff members in the banks, making them aware about the actual meaning and use of this perception. Table 4.2 shows the t-test conducted for the sample. As per Table, all the values anticipate statement facility and loan services are significant. According to hypothesis H_0 all the selected attributes affects customer satisfaction equally while the finding of current research shows that the relationship of customers with manager/ customer relationship officer (mean = 27.57) affects customer satisfaction the most.

Further, this research shows that private banks managers are to the lead of public banks in making relationship with their customer thus winning their satisfaction. This can be attributed to the fact that today larger client base in Manipur view that public sector banks are lagging behind in use of modern technology and techno savvy staff. According to the finding, there is no difference in satisfaction level of customer in public and private banks but the findings of current research shows that private sector banks are providing better services in terms of query resolution through telephone, branch facilities, services by teller and above all customer relations with manager (all the significant t-values taken). Thus hypothesis H_0 is rejected.

This research shows that if the facilities in the branch, viz. infrastructure, ambience, décor, sitting facility, signage etc. are adequate, it not only leads to customer satisfaction but overall improvement in working of the branch as well whether it is services by teller, managers, loan services. If all the signage are in place it will direct the customer to right desk without wasting their time which further helps the service officer in attending to the customers in time and providing to their needs. Table 4.3 shows correlation of attributes viz. services offered by teller, relationship with manager, branch facilities, loan services and enquiry on telephone for measuring customer satisfaction. According to the finding, all the selected attributes of customer satisfaction are uncorrelated while our finding shows that all the attributes apart from loan services are correlated. Thus alternative hypothesis HA is accepted.

References

Akbar, Syed Asad (1990). "Bank Marketing—Some Issues", *IOB MNR*, Vol.4, No. 12, pp. 20-22.

Aurora, S. and Malhotra, M. (1997). 'Customer Satisfaction: A Comparative Analysis of Public and Private Sector Bank', *Decision*, Vol. 24, No. 1-4, January-December, pp. 109-130.

Bhatt, A. (1990). "Study of Marketing Research in Banking", *NIBM*, Pune, p. 5.

Bitner, M.J. and Hubbert, A.R. (1994). "Encounter Satisfaction Versus Overall Satisfaction Versus Quality; The Customer Voice", in Rust, R.T., and Oliver, R.C. (Eds.), *Service Quality, New Directions in Theory and Practice*, Sage Publications, C.A., London, New Delhi, pp. 72-94.

Bolton, R.N. and Drew, J.H. (1994), "Linking Customers Satisfaction to Service Operations and Outcomes", in Rust, R.T., and Oliver, R.C. (Eds), *Service Quality, New Directions in Theory and Practice*, Sage Publications, C.A., London, New Delhi, pp. 173-201.

Boyd, W.L., Leonard, M. and White, C. (1994), "Customer Preferences for Financial Services: An Analysis", *International Journal of Bank Marketing*, Vol. 12, No. 1, pp. 9-15.

Dutt, K. and Dutta, A. (2009), "Customers Expectation and Perception Across the Indian Banking Industry and the Resultant Financial Implications", *Journal of Services Research*, Vol. 9, No. 1, pp. 31-49.

Geiger, H. (1975). "Standard Surveys for Analyzing Local Bank Competition". In "The Use of Market Research in Financial Fields", *ESOMAR*. pp. 85-95.

Hallowell Roger (1996). "The Relationships of Customer Satisfaction, Customer Loyalty and Profitability: An Empirical Study". *International Journal Of Service Industry Management*. Vol. 7, No. 4, pp. 27-42.

Huu Phuong Ta, Kar Yin Har (2000). "A Study of Bank Selection Decisions In Singapore Using the Analytical Hierarchy Process". *The International Journal of Bank Marketing*, Vol. 18, No. 4, pp. 170-180.

Laroche, M., Rosenblatt, J.A., and Manning, T. (1986). "Services Used and Factors Considered Important in Selecting a Bank: An Investigation Across Diverse Demographic Segments". *International Journal of Bank Marketing*, Vol. 4 (1), pp. 35-55.

Lewis, B.R. and Birmingham, G.H. (1991). 'The Youth Market for Financial Services'. *International Journal of Bank Marketing*, Vol. 9(2). pp. 3-11.

Liang Chhiung-Ju and Wang Wen-Hung. (2004). "Attributes, Benefits, Customer Satisfaction and Behavioural Loyalty—An Integrative Research of Financial Services Industry in Taiwan". *Journal of Services Research*, Vol. 4, No. 1, April-September. pp. 23-57.

Meidan, A. (1976). "Branch Manager's Attitude on Bank Objectives and Operations". *Proceedings of the European Academy of Advanced Research in Marketing Conference*, France, pp. 215-228.

Nair, Rajagopala. (1994). *Rural Bank Marketing in Kerala*, unpublished doctoral dissertation, University of Kerala.

Nirmaljeet Virk and Prabhjot Kaur Mahal (2013). "Customer Satisfaction: A Comparative Analysis of Public and Private Sector Banks in India". *KAIM Journal of Management and Research*, Vol. 6, No.1, May-October, pp.75-80.

Sarin, Anil (2007). "Contemporary Issues in Services Marketing", *Indian Journal of Marketing*. Vol. 37, pp. 40-44.

Smith, Anne M. (1990). 'Quality Aspects of Services Marketing', *Marketing Intelligence & Planning*, Vol. 8, No. 6.

Tyler, K. and Stanley, E. (2001). "Corporate Banking: the Strategic Impact of Boundary ICBI 2010—University of Kelaniya, Sri Lanka Spanner Effectiveness". *International Journal of Bank Marketing*, Vol. 19 (6), pp. 246-252.

Books

Maheshwari, S.N. and Maheshwari, S.K. (1979). *Banking Law and Practices*, 12th edition, Kalyani Publishers, New Delhi.

Walsh, W.B. (1995). *Tests and Assessment*, 3rd edition, Prentice Hall, New Jersey.

5

Consumer Welfare through Consumer's Equilibrium in Monopolistic Daily Newspaper Publishers in Manipur

Huidrom Imobi Singh and *Adaso Lophro*

Introduction

Consumers are the individuals who belong to largest economic agent in the society. The welfare of consumer means the welfare of humanity. All the human beings are consumer provided the income, taste and preferences, prices of other goods in general and the particular price and quality of the goods. The terminology of consumer's equilibrium is conducive and/or correlate to consumer welfare. At one particular point, he/she is getting the maximum satisfaction from the consumption of the goods. Consumer welfare is a more complex and integrated term. The welfare given by newspapers under monopolistic competition through Consumer's equilibrium model will be the present interesting topic of concern in the context of Manipur. There are 33 local dailies published in Manipur out of which 9 are in English language and others in their own mother tongue. The average maximum circulations per day among the daily newspapers are *Poknapham* and *Sangai Express*.

Both of these papers are having English and Manipuri editions. *Sangai Express* English edition is very popular and maximum circulation in Valley and hill areas of Manipur. *Poknapham*, the Manipuri edition, is famous in Valley areas. These two are very competitive daily newspapers containing varieties of information and advertisement. Because of price differentiation, contents, quality and the pages of the newspapers, the market of such kind will be monopolistic competition in nature. In such type of imperfect market, consumer satisfaction will be the highest and the choice of the consumer is perfect.

Objectives of the Study

1. To analyse the consumer's equilibrium.
2. To examine the content of information and welfare service given by Daily Newspapers.
3. To analyze the price, buyers and sellers in the market.

Consumer's Equilibrium and Newspapers

The maximum satisfaction that the consumers are getting from the reading of various newspapers published in Manipur can be examined through the content of information and price of the newspapers. Newspapers are playing an important role for dynamic knowledge-driven economy. They have been supplying the dynamic information to the consumers and the economy is moving upward from the satisfaction and knowledge of information. Everyday we are reading newspaper and we get the knowledge and information of various kinds making our self-perfect information, ultimately reaching the equilibrium point. The time, cost and energy I incurred at one side and the content of information and knowledge I got from the other side always estimated for my welfare. The two forces interact, the demand and supply force, and then determine the equilibrium of the consumers. Some consumers are reading only one favourite newspaper and some are reading a combination of two or more depending on his income and preferences. They are reading various contents of the papers that giving him maximum satisfaction. Therefore, the consumer is in equilibrium with the consumption of one or many newspapers. He is reading many articles on social issues, sport events, Gas news, advertisement, current events and many more information from the newspapers.

Some Newspapers having Maximum Circulation in Manipur

1. The *Sangai Express* is the most popular news agency in Manipur. It is available in English and Manipuri languages. Features of its publication are: (i) Coverage of sensitive social issues. (ii) Exclusive general article including research article, religious topics, events in the ethnic community and international events. (iii) Special coverage of sports: It has a separate and dedicated section for covering all the events in sports taking place around the world. (iv) Advertisement on various occasions.
2. *Poknapham and the people chronicle:* Features of its publication are: (i) Coverage of sensitive social issues. (ii) Exclusive general article including research article, religious topics, events in the ethnic community and international events. (iii) Special coverage of sports—It has a separate and dedicated section for covering the events in sports taking place around the world. (iv) Advertisement on economic and commercial services.
3. *Hueiyen lanpao* is well known for its initiative edition in Meitei Mayak. It is printed in three different languages, i.e. Manipuri, English and Meitei Mayak. It is also one of the most circulated newspapers in Imphal and valley area.
4. *Naharolgi Thoudang* is famous about its editorial notes and is printed in Manipuri language. It is a newspaper dedicated to the cause of human rights. Valley people are most interested on this paper.
5. *Sana Leibak* is popular for its dedicated service on holidays. It is the only daily newspaper published throughout the year (365 days) in Manipuri edition.

6. *The Imphal Free Press*, English daily since 1996 took the state by storm when it hit the news stand with a modern touch.

Table 5.1: List of local dailies in Manipur (as on 15th October, 2017)

Sl. No.	Daily Newspaper	Editors	Average circulation/ price
1	Aja - Tangkhul	Valley Rose	3000/Rs. 4
2	The Cham - Kabui	Ramkung Panmei	5000/Rs.3
3	Eimi Times - Kuki & English	David letgoulien Gangte	6000/Rs.
4	Hueiyen lanpao - Meitei	Hamanta Kumar	Rs.
5	Hueiyen lanpao - Manipuri	Hamanta Kumar	27,287/Rs.
6	Hueiyen lanpao - English	Dhiren A. Sadokpam	26,424/Rs.
7	Hmasawnnathar - Hmar	Lalmalsawm Sellate	6,000/Rs.5
8	Hills Hornbill Express - English	Peter Adani	2000 above/ Rs. 3
9	Ireibak - Manipuri	Laishram Kumar	Rs.
10	Ichel Express	Irengbam Arun	Rs.
11	Imphal free press - English	Pradip Phanjoubam	5,400/Rs. 3
12	Imphal Times - Eng/Eve	Rinku Khumukcham	Rs.
13	Kangla Pao - Manipuri/Eve	P. Ibochouba	Rs.
14	Kangleipakki Meira – do-	W. Shyamjai	Rs.
15	Lamka post - Paite	Th. Thangzalian	Rs.
16	Manipur Express - Paite	L. Chinkhanlian	Rs.
17	Manipur mail - English	N Sanatomba	24,727/Rs.
18	Mannaba - Manipuri/eve	Ch Megabarna	Rs.
19	Meeyam - Manipuri/eve	S. Jugol	Rs.
20	Manipur Chronicle - English	Nilotpol Choudhury	Rs.
21	Nisin Thuhiltu - Vaiphei	Vicky Suantak	Rs.
22	Naharolgi Thoudang	Khoirom Loyalakpa	47,910/ Rs. 3.60
23	Poknapham - Manipuri	A. Robindro Sharma	58,000/ Rs. 4.50

(*Contd.*)

Sl. No.	Daily Newspaper	Editors	Average circulation/ price
24	People's Chronicle- English	G. Bhabesh Candra	20,000/Rs. 4.50
25	Paojel – Manipuri/eve	Ranjit Oinamcha	Rs.
26	Pandam - Manipuri	Ch Khumanleima chanu	Rs.
27	Sangi Express - Manipuri	Khogendra Khomdram	56,564/Rs. 4.50
28	Sangi Express - English	Hijam Rajesh	Rs.
29	Sanaleibak - Manipuri	H Achouba Shrama	Rs.3
30	Thoudok Wathok- Manipur	Sh Umeshchandra	Rs.
31	The Dawn Tantak - Tangkhul	Addie Chiphang	Rs.
32	Zogam Today – Zou	S. Nengkhanlun	3000 and above/Rs.4
33	Herald Today - English	John Basho	Less than 1000/Rs.3

Source: 1. Government of Manipur, directorate of information and public relation.
2. Direct Personal investigation, have used telephone interview (Circulation).

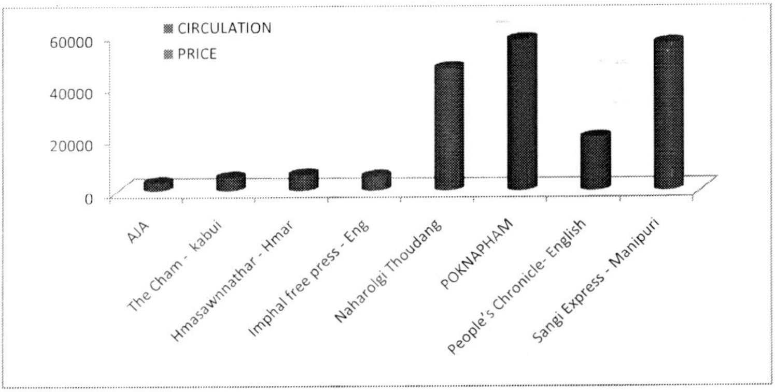

Fig. 5.1: Diagram showing the circulations of some of the local dailies newspapers in Manipur

The Interaction of Consumers and Producers

The market demand for newspapers is derived from the individual reader of newspaper and most influential with the price and contents. Price and contents are directly related, high price of newspapers is because of the contents and *vice versa*. In the papers of *Sangai Express* and *Poknapham* advertising contents are distinguishing features from the other newspapers. Generally, the newsreader in Manipur used to buy these two newspapers because of advertisement content, maximum coverage of other socio-economic issues and the moderate price. They are charging Rs.4.50 per paper on 16/12 multi-colour pages, which is reasonable in Manipur context. There are other newspapers whose prices and content are less than these two newspapers. *Naharolgi Thoudang*, *The Imphal Free Press*, *Huiyen Lanpao* and *Sana Leipak* (only newspapers having no holiday in Manipur) are the newspapers in the second order of people preference. Consumers can decide their maximum satisfaction and try to reach his welfare through the reading of one newspaper or, combination of two or more newspapers. The market supply curve of producer is linked with the demand of the consumer and according to their price and contents of the newspapers. Aggregate demand is more influencing factor for making reasonable profits and maximum supply. Aggregate demand is composed of individual demand, institutional demand, government demand and export demand. The producers compare his average revenue (demand curve) and average cost (treat as supply curve) and determine the profits, ultimately the marginal revenue and marginal cost for additional sale. In modern economy, producers are thinking about the business profit at one side and service satisfaction on the other. Here lies the interaction of consumers and producers. It is very important to the producers to know the behaviour of consumers for sustainable service and production. "How to give maximum welfare to the consumers", should be in the mind and critical issues for every publisher in modern context. This question is very much connected to monopolistic markets otherwise; they cannot get the market share. It is also equally important to the producers or publishers about the people (consumers) comment regarding the contents of information of the newspapers. The objective of monopolistic competition is met by ensuring that there are sufficient numbers of producers so that no producer can attain a position of dominance. The nature of this industry is the dominance in terms of market share, which is very important. Therefore, it seeks to ensure that there is no abuse to the consumers because of this dominance.

For instance, a dominant newspaper says, *Phoknapham* or *Sangai Express English,* that is able to attract new customers on the basis of an innovative idea, content and information might thereby "disadvantage" rivals because it reduces demand for their products and leads them to compete less aggressively. The dominant publishers should be encouraged to compete aggressively on the merits and with the consideration of welfare of readers. So in a market having large number of buyers and sellers of newspapers with differentiated products get the advantage of making consumer welfare maximum.

Suggestions

1. The newspapers should be unique in character, which means many newspapers published are copied from each other. To avoid these issues of similarity of news should be taken care of, not monopolizing from others news.
2. The publisher should avoid causality of information of publishing news.
3. The publisher should give variety of information without any partiality irrespective of Caste, Creed and Politics.
4. The newspapers should provide clearcut information regarding policy and programme of the government for the betterment of the consumers.

Conclusion

The welfare service given by daily newspapers to the consumers for various kinds of information is really great and considerable. They are certainly giving an injection of ideas and particular influential knowledge to the community. Consumers are enlightened through various kinds of information. However, the publication of newspapers should be original and real service of the society not for profit motives only. It demands.

The interaction between the reader and advertising markets on the one side, the publisher and the advertising market on the other is rather complex and these two monopolistic industries are having different objectivity. It leads, however, to an important conclusion: under advertisement-attraction, concentration in the press industry should be expected as a direct and natural consequence of the advertising market. Since newspapers constitute a major vehicle for spreading political and social information to citizens, it is important to recognize the shortcomings in the business model that might lead to high concentration. One direction for future research is to take a deeper look at actual market structures. Most systems are mixed, and it includes a variety of different firm types.

References

Athey, S. and M. Mobius (2012). "The Impact of News Aggregators on Internet News Consumption: The Case of Localization," *Working paper.*

Calzada, J. and G. Ordóñez (2012). "Competition in the news industry: fighting aggregators with versions and links," *Working Papers* 12-22, NET Institute.

Doh-Shin Jeony and Nikrooz Nasrz, *News Aggregators and Competition Among Newspapers on the Internet,* July 16, 2014.

Erik Brynjolfsson, *The Contribution of Information Technology for Consumers Welfare,* Sloan School of Management, MIT, Camdridge, Massachusetts 02139.

Gabszewicz, J.J., D. Laussel, and N. Sonnac (2001). "Press advertising and the ascent of the 'Pensée Unique'," *European Economic Review, 45*(4-6), 641-651.

Government of Manipur, directorate of information and public relation.

Gregory Sidak J., "A Consumer-welfare Approach to Network Neutrality Regulation of the Internet", *Journal of Competition Law and Economics, 2*(3), 349-474.

Lee, Yoon-Ho Alex (2006). "Competition, Consumer Welfare, and the Social Cost of Monopoly" *Student Scholarship Papers.* Paper 19.

6

Consumer Rights and Government

Manipur Context

Th. Binarani Devi

Introduction

Consumer right is linked with consumer protection and the formation of consumer organizations, which help consumer, make better choices in the marketplace and get help with consumer complaints. Other organizations that promote consumer protection include government and governmental organizations and self-regulating business organizations such as consumer protection agencies and organizations. As an independent citizen of free India, consumers of Manipur also have full rights to choose any product according to his/her choice and services related with the product of his/her choice at competitive prices with assurance of satisfactory quality.

Consumer and Consumer Rights

A consumer is a person who is buying goods for his personal use or consumption and not for any other purposes. He is the ultimate buyer or customer. Consumer buying behaviour refers specifically to the actions consumers take when deciding what to buy and when making actual behaviour[1]. People do not buy any product but rather solutions to problems or good feelings. The consumer has the right to choose any product according to his/her choice and services related with the available product of his/her choice at competitive prices with assurance of satisfactory quality. Before purchasing any commodity, consumer should think about what he/she wants the product to do and its consequences. He can shop around any market at any place for the best deal by comparing quality, design, and prices, even for the same goods. After choosing any goods, he can ask for advice about the goods and even for uses of the goods and its value or importance to the retailer or producer. After finalizing to buy the goods he should inspect goods carefully and need to keep all invoices, dockets and receipts from the retailer or the stockist or even producer. If things go wrong in spite of such precautions, and one is sure that the buyer did not cause any fault, stop buying the faulty goods. Let the seller know as soon as possible about the problem and let the retailer or the producer acknowledge that the buyers have the capacity to know the problems or defects or not satisfied with the service or products or its consequences.

Consumer rights are generally a reference to a body of law that pertains to things the producers of goods must do to protect customers from harm. Consumer right is a civil right of an independent citizen of an independent country. This is right to basic goods and services which guarantee survival, adequate food, clothing, shelter, healthcare, education and sanitation. It can protect against the marketing of goods or the provision of services that are hazardous to health and life information and again, the right to be protected against dishonest or misleading advertising or labelling. And the right to be given the fact and information needed to make an informed choice. Consumer right is the type of rights which support the right to express consumer interest in the making and executing of government policies and to be compensated for misrepresentation, shoddy goods or deficient or unsatisfactory services. Consumer has the right to acquire the knowledge and skills necessary to be an informed consumer. All the people should have the right to live and work in an environment which is neither threatening nor dangerous and which permits a life of dignity and well-being. There is an urgent need for spreading awareness of the rights of the consumers. Legally, the buyers have the power to return the faulty goods as soon as he can. If the return goods are too large to handle, he should write detail to the seller about the problem. Give details of the fault and what you want to do about it. In such cases the customer need to show proof of purchase for example, a receipt or a credit card slip. The buyer needs to ask to see the manager or the owner. If the buyer could not see someone in authority, need to write a letter first by explaining the problem calmly and clearly. If the buyer leaves the goods with the store, make sure you get a receipt. Make sure you look after the goods while they are still in your care.

In 1985, the United Nations General Assembly adopted eight basic consumer rights which resulted in consumers having stronger consumer protection policies worldwide.

1. *The Right to Choose*—Within reason, consumers has the rights to be assured that a selection of quality products and services are available for them to purchase at competitive prices. It means that a consumer should have the opportunity to select the goods or services that he or she wants to purchase.
2. *The Right to Safety*—Consumers have the right to expect protection from hazardous products and services purchased in the market place, particularly if used properly for their intended purpose. Consumers have protection from the sale and distribution of dangerous goods and services.
3. *The Right to be Informed*—Consumers have the rights to receive adequate information about products on which to base buying decisions. Reliable sources exist to inform consumers about products or services.
4. *The Rights to be Heard and the Right to Voice*—Consumers have the right to equal and fair consideration in government policy making situation, as well as prompt treatment

in administrative courts or legal communities. In other words, consumers have a right to complain when there are problems or concerns. They have the right to speak up, to be heard, and to expect positive result. Through this right, both business and government are expected to respond to consumers.

5. *The Right to Redress or Remedy*— Consumers are afforded an opportunity to have a hearing to voice dissatisfaction such that a resolution is reached and the complaint is settled satisfactorily.
6. *The Right to Environmental Health*—Consumers should be protected from the devastating effects of air, earth and water pollution that may result from the performance of daily marketplace operations. Consumers have the right to live and work in an environment that does not threaten the well-being of present and future generations.
7. *The Right to Service*—Consumers may expect convenience, the right to be treated with respect, an appropriate response to their needs and problems, and good quality design and workmanship in a product. Additionally, consumers may expect a courteous manner while in a store or other establishment even if a purchase is not made. Service means access to essential goods and services to include adequate food shelter, clothing, healthcare, education and sanitation—basic needs that should be available to all consumers.
8. *The Right to Consumer Education*—Consumers are extended the right to continuing consumer education that support the benefits and enjoyment of other specific rights. Consumers have the right to some form of training and mastery of knowledge and skills needed to make improved decisions in the market place.

Customer *versus* Producer or Retailer

Development of any society depends upon the capacity for the exchange of goods and services at different levels—local, state, national and international. For exchanging the goods under barter system the retailers, factory owners, producers, industrialists etc. are taking a king pin role. A retailer, factory owner, producer, industrialist etc. produces goods and give fulfilment and satisfaction to the consumer and get profit out of it. They use different techniques for selling their goods. Most of the retailers' activities deliver a force of services to the consumer, creating assortments at competitive prices in accessible locations. These activities, therefore, all play major roles in creating customer satisfaction[2]. With the continuous rise in the purchasing power of the public in general and the middle class in particular, the transaction and consumption of goods and services have been increasing dramatically. Consumers are also affected by their own psychological influences, by a variety of socio-cultural influences, and unique situational influences that apply to each purchase. Consumers live in complex social environments which are varied from society to society and from time to time. The kind of products they buy can be influenced by the culture they grew up in, by demographic factors such as their age, income, by their social status, by their household make up, by the groups they belong, and by the people they know[3]. Goods available in the market are according to the variation of place and season. Retailers and e-retailers now specify (and sometimes design) products to a much greater extent than previously, reflecting closeness to the consumer and appreciation of benefits that consumers want[4]. Some retailers or producers primarily concern is only with their profit and not in the interest of the customer. In connection with the profit of the retailers or producers, advertisement has a great role. Advertisement is not bad at all; it can give certain messages or benefits to the consumers also by giving the importance of the goods, changes, modification or upgradation of the products. A customer is generally misled by star or model studded advertisement. Advertisement creates a void in the mind of customer. A customer is often cheated by purchasing less weighing commodity or purchase of inferior or sometime injurious commodity, purchase of duplicated or expiry dated goods or paying more prices than MRP. In Manipur, sometimes, purchase of goods on more than MRP is done due to compulsion of bandh, strike, extortion, landslides etc. In certain cases, consumers are so careless and not ready to take care of their rights. Most of the customers, even educated ones, do not think or know that they can bargain on MRP price as well.

Consumer Culture in Manipur

At present, the state of Manipur has no capacity for producing enough food for its home consumption on the other hand with the increasing expansion of the wave of globalization, consumer culture is all pervasive. With India's Look East Policy/Act East Policy, Manipur becames a part of global market. All the companies, including the multinationals reached every nook and corner of the state. They have expanded their business with middlemen at every level. The entire market system of Manipur works to meet all the current needs of ultimate/final buyers even though there is no big industry or factory. Market functions mainly on twin factors—producers and customers. In between producers and consumers there are many market players as intermediary or agents or wholesaler or retailers/hawker. In limited cases, sometimes, produced goods or commodities may be sold directly while in most cases commodities are sold by simply change of hands or by value addition. Sometimes more consumption is equated wrongly with consumerism. More consumption is becoming now-a-days a symbol of one's status while consumerism refers to consumer movements, a movement to protect consumer rights. The customers are well aware and acknowledge everything about the goods that have certain problems, until and unless they are compelled to buy goods due to unavoidable circumstances. Typical gloomy socio-political and geographical scenario created typical market situation too. Economic road blockade of more than hundred days on the national highways by the civil society organizations, landslides, mud flow etc. threaten the consumers of Manipur for their basic needs. Hoarding, black marketing, influence of money lenders etc.

are the weapons used by the traders and businessmen during such conditions. People used to buy cooking gas cylinder @Rs. 2,500, petrol @Rs. 399 per litre, onion @Rs. 100 per kg etc. during such period. Online shopping and marketing is becoming one of the upcoming fashions for buying goods in this global society. When buying online, consumers as far less likely to request help than they are in the store. Rather e-shoppers who need help in understanding a product are more likely to abandon the transaction and find an alternative supplier or even buy through a different channel[5]. Retailer, wholesalers, middlemen etc. are taking benfit of this situation. All the retailers or wholesalers are trying to catch the customer by any means.

Government for the Protection of Consumer Rights

If the consumer and seller or service provider cannot agree on certain points in connection with buying or returning any goods, the consumer can seek advice from some consumer courts or small cause's courts. While filing a complaint in the consumer forum, it is essential that the aggrieved consumer must know in which consumer district he or she belongs. A consumer jurisdiction is the technical legal issue and filing a complaint in the forum which does not have a jurisdiction lead to rejection of the complaint. If there is a fair amount of money involved, the buyer may prefer to get advice from a lawyer or a relevant organization. Now-a-days, consumers are also forming groups in connection with the use of certain commodities. A consumer structure is organized around the country. This structure is useful where different types of producers might produce different products in different quantities, or have different needs or imitations are coming up. They (producers) jointly need to find out the problems and highlight the realities, above their interest of profit. They are more powerful than the individual customer. If problems are there, they can contact the producer and other related persons. The last resort is to go to court.

The main duty of the government of any country is the welfare and development of the society; by providing all the basic needs of the subjects of the society. Again, the government will have to take care about the provisions, availability, disposal, uses etc of all the basic needs. Protection of the rights of the consumer is also one of the basic duties of the government. The Government of India also took up different steps for the protection of the rights of consumers with different Laws, Regulations, Acts, Bills etc., which covers all the states and Union Territories.

In order to prevent unethical trade practices like hoarding and black-marketing etc., the Prevention of Black-marketing of Supplies of Essential Commodities Act, 1980 is being implemented by the government to detain persons whose activities are found to be prejudicial to the maintenance of supplies of commodities essential to the community. This is an Act to provide the detention in certain cases for the purpose of black marketing and maintenance of supplies of commodities essential to the community and for the matter therewith.

Consumer Protection Act, 1986 is an Act to provide for the better protection of the interest of consumers and for that purpose to make provisions for the establishment of Consumer Councils and other authorities for the settlement of consumers' disputes and for matters connected therewith.

The Consumer Protection Act lays down framework for ensuring that the violations of consumer rights are properly dealt with. But efficient and appropriate consumer protection is possible only when the consumers themselves are well aware of their rights in the first place. There is need for the involvement and awareness of their rights as a consumer by the public. People don't protest or raise their voice in case of denial of their rights. Government has provided ration cards for each household for their daily basic needs. People get ration cards from the concerned Deputy Commissioner. When there is any case of missing the ration card or any malpractice in connection with the supply of goods, people rarely come forward or knock the doors of the DC's office to demand their ration cards. Even those few lucky who are having ration cards would not complain when their quotas are reduced by the Fair

Price Shop agents. Many possess APL cards but just a few of them come up to claim their rights with vigour due to lack of awareness of the consumer's rights or lack of confidence in the grievance redressal mechanism. Both the ruling and opposition parties of the government try to politicalize the matter and try to influence the consumers in the electioneering process. Manipur State Consumer Dispute Redressal Commission has been designated as the State Food Commission to look into the grievances of the National Food Safety Act. The beneficiaries may lodge their complaints online through *pdsmanipur.noc.in*. The Consumer Courts do not charge any court fee. Like in the usual case, the complainant can appear himself, through a lawyer or a registered consumer protection organization. Under the Consumer Protection Act, the cases received by these courts are solved/disposed within three months of receiving the complaints.

District Consumer Dispute Reddressal Forum in Manipur received the complaints involving cost and compensation more than twenty lakh for receiving help from the state Consumer Redressal Commission or National Consumer Dispute Redressal Commission. The bench at the District Forum and State Commission consist of a President and two nominated members, male and female. The President of this forum is usually a District or High Court Judge. The decision of these members is final. The National Commission has five members bench, the President being a Supreme Court Judge, and four other members, one of them being a nominated lady member.

If it is believed that the consumer right of any person is violated and it resulted harm to others, that person may wish to speak to the attorney. Even if the individual harm of that person is not that great, the cumulative base may be staggering. Thus, if anybody is able to initiate a class action suit, that person may be able to affect real change and help to prevent others from harm.

Consumer complaints can be filed according to the value of the compensation required. If the value is up to Rs. 20,00,000 the consumer should complain to the District Forum; value is between Rs. 20,00,000 to Rs. 1 crore it should complain to the State Consumer Dispute Redressal Commission; and value is above Rs. 1 crore it should complain to the National Consumer Redressal Commission, New Delhi. The complainant can present his or her authorized representative to the District Forum or State Commission. This complaint can be sent by registered post to the respective forum. Five copies of the complaint have to be taken—One for each member (3), one for opposite party, and one for the complainant. An additional copy for each opposite has to be filed. The complainant should retain his copy while filing the complaint or any authorized person can do the same with an authorized letter. The time frame is within two years of receiving the last correspondence, letters, notice, acknowledgment etc. There is always one option of appealing to the higher court. The time frame for complaint to the State Commission is within 30 days against order of District Forum. The same applies to each level. Consumer complaints can be filed against the manufacturer or provider of goods and services, value adders, retailer traders etc. but it should be noted that a consumer complaint cannot be filed against providers of free goods and services.

World Consumers Rights Day is observed all over the world on 15 March to recognize the rights of the people as consumers. The Consumer Rights Organization was founded on March 15, 1960 and two years later on 15 March, 1962, US President John F. Kennedy gave his speech on Consumer Rights. The World Consumers Rights Day was first observed in 1963.

Manipur state government also takes care of the consumer rights by providing support and creating an environment for establishing a society that seek to protect the rights of consumers and taking punitive actions against the unscrupulous services and goods providers. Manipur State Consumer Dispute Redressal Commission is one of such organization. Another important intervention for the protection of consumer's right is the State Consumer Helpline which is functioning under the watch of CAF and PD Department.

Conclusion

In Manipur people are not so aware of the rights as a consumer. But the problems and issue of consumers' right is touching its limit. The state is an underdeveloped state and all the basic provisions are coming from other states of India and her neighbouring countries. Different companies, including multi-nationals are searching their markets for selling their products. Manipur is one of their targeted places. Consumer culture of this state is also something different. The geo-political and social condition of the state is also quite typical. Only three hours rainfall resulted landslides and closed roads which are lifelines of the people. Any accident occurred in any part of the highways, bandh is called by the victim party. During such bandhs blockades and landslides the prices of the commodities skyrocket. They check the prices and qualities of the goods. In one sense that actions of these civil society organizations are good but controversy between the retailers and these civil society organizations are common. So, if the government takes steps by using all the related staffs such incidents will not happen. And the public also need to be aware and consider their rights and need not be so hasty in buying goods beyond their budget. Awareness programmes should be organized by giving information to the public. Only observation of consumers' rights days is not enough for the protection of consumers' rights. It is necessary to discuss why such groups are coming out in spite of the activities of the existing government with different Acts and laws and how to protect the rights of the consumers.

Notes

1. J.N. Jain, P.P. Singh, and S.K. Bhatia, *Modern Marketing Management—Principles and Techniques*, Regal Publications, New Delhi, p. 139.
2. Gautam Bansal and Sandhar Sharma, *Retail Management*, IB Publication and Distribution, New Delhi, p. 246.
3. J.N Jain, P.P. Singh, and S.K Bhatia, *op cit.,* p. 150.
4. Gautam Bansal and Sandhar Sharma, *op cit.,* p. 248.
5. *Ibid.*

7

Role of Consumer Disputes Redressal Commissions in India

G.P. Prasain and *John Mang Muan Lian Zou*

Introduction

The protection of consumer's interest has been one of the main priorities taken up at the central as well as state level in India since India's Independence. Since the introduction of Sale of Goods Act in 1930, the government has made numerous laws and acts for the protection of consumer rights. Prominent among these legislations are[1]: The Drugs Control Act, 1950; Industries (Development and Regulation) Act, 1951; the Indian Standards Institution (Certification Marks) Act, 1952; the Drugs and Magic Remedies (Objectionable Advertisements) Act, 1954; the Prevention of Food Adulteration Act, 1954; the Essential Commodities Act, 1955; the Trade and Merchandise Marks Act, 1958; the Essential Services Maintenance Act, 1968; the Monopolies and Restrictive Trade Practices Act, 1969; the Maintenance of Internal Security Act, 1971; the Hire Purchase Act, 1972; the Cigarettes (Regulation of Production, Supply and Distribution) Act, 1975; the Standards of Weights and Measures Act, 1976; the Prevention of Black Marketing and Maintenance of Essential Commodities Act, 1980; the Standard of Weights and Measures (Enforcement) Act, 1985; the Narcotics Drugs and Psychotropic Substances Act, 1985; the Bureau of Indian Standards Act, 1986; and the Consumer Protection Act, 1986 etc.

The emergence of the new consumer protection movement owes its origin primarily to the enactment and implementation of the Consumer Protection Act, 1986. The 1986 Act envisages a unique Three-Tier Quasi-Judicial Consumer Disputes Redressal Mechanism, with a District Consumer Disputes Redressal Forum (DCDRF) at the lowest level, a State Consumer Disputes Redressal Commission (SCDRC) at the middle level, and the National Consumer Disputes Redressal Commission (NCDRC) at the apex level. In addition to this, Three-Tier Consumer Disputes Redressal Fora, there is also a provision for the establishment of the Consumer Protection Councils at the district, state and the national levels with the sole aim of protecting consumer interest in the market place.

Significance of the Study

A lot of issues have come for adjudication before the National Consumer Disputes Redressal Commission during the course of its decision-making. It is heartening to know that the National Commission has made its presence felt on the scenario and has always stood for the consumers, thereby delivering their interests from time to time. Many a time crisis does arise whenever a controversial issue came up for adjudication before the apex Commission, be it the applicability of the Consumer Protection Act, 1986 to the educational services, or to the housing industry, or to the legal profession as well as to the medical profession. There is no denying the fact that the National Commission has handled all such situations in a mature and a proper manner and by way of pronouncing certain absorbing judgments. The Commission has brought these services within the ambit and jurisdiction of the Consumer Protection Act, 1986. Calls for consumer protection legislation are often motivated by a claim that buyers are in some sense weaker than sellers in the marketplace. Given such circumstance, active consumer protection is desirable either as a device for increasing equity among buyers and sellers or as a method for improving the efficiency of marketing activities.

Objectives of the Study

This chapter attempts to understand the concept of consumer dispute and workings of the Redressal Agencies; who can file a complaint and the procedure of filing a complaint, findings and powers of redressal agencies, how to appeal against the order of Redressal Agencies. The various types of penalties which can be imposed by the Redressal Agency due to non-acceptance of their orders.

Review of Literature

A.K. Saxenaa (1978), in his article, analyses and compares the Indian and Western consumerism. He opines that major causes for consumerism in India are: soaring prices; poor and sub-standard products and service performance, inadequate production, gross adulteration, arbitrary weight and measures, deceptive advertising and publicity campaign.

Vijendra B. Khamesra (1980), article deals with consumer protection in India and stresses that the Indian consumer needs to be educated about his rights, as has been done in the USA Consumer Protection is possible in India, but effective enforcement by legislation and a sustained drive to educate the people are necessary.

G.N. Sahu (1981), in his article explains that consumerism concerns the entire society as everybody is a consumer of some kind or the other of goods/services. According to him, the problems of consumers in India are: over charge, underweight, adulteration, imitation, defective packing and bad services by fraudulent, deceptive, unethical and unscrupulous businessmen. The problems are accentuated by illiteracy, ignorance and lack of awareness of the majority of Indian consumers about their rights. Consumers can be relieved of this menacing problem, if both the government and general public join hands with all sincerity.

D.A.R. Subramanyam (1982), found in his study, to elicit the opinion of educated consumers in Gwatur district of Andhra Pradesh, that a large majority of persons became aware of the terms such as 'consumer', 'consumer protection' and 'consumer movement' quite late and that too through newspapers and magazines. About a quarter of the respondents came to know about these terms during their casual discussions with their friends.

H.C. Chaudhary (1982), in his article offers a penetrating insight into the issues involved in the consumer protection moment. He explains that the government, business and society shall find it useful in enlightening themselves of the emerging forces emanating from the buying side of business and understanding the social, political, economic and psychological aspects of Indian consumers' movements.

Sharmila Thakur (1992), in her study observed that executives recognized business failings in the area of advertisements, complaint processing and pricing, but felt that government intervention was necessary in order to protect consumers. Students seemed to be more concerned about consumer problems like inadequate product information and adulteration besides complaint redressal; however, they were not favourably inclined towards the idea of government regulations, i.e. business. Instead they seemed to prefer self-regulation, thus upholding the marketing concept.

Kiran Singh (1992) conducted a study of consumer awareness in Hissar district and it was found that consumer awareness about consumer protection legislation was lacking among both the rural and urban population. The study reveals that almost all people in rural areas and nearly 90 per cent of urban population had never heard of any consumer protection legislation.

O.P. Garg's book "*The Consumer Protection Act, 1986*" deals with the subject of consumer protection in a historical retrospect and shows stage by stage the development of law relating to consumer movement in the country. The book is quite helpful to both the consumers and the producers.

Gurbax Singh (1992), in his book "*Law of Consumer Protection*", traces the development of consumer protection movement and the history of consumer legislations in different countries of the western world and briefly summarises the objects of consumer laws and the importance of consumer guidance. It includes model petition of complaint and appealed for the guidance of consumers.

Gurbax Singh's (1993) book "*Law of Consumer Protection*" traces the development of consumer protection movement and the history of consumer legislations in different countries of the Western World and briefly summarise the objects of consumer laws and the importance of consumer guidance. It includes model petition of complaint and appeal etc. for the guidance of consumers. It also provides comprehensive information on all aspects of the consumer protection and is of great assistance, value and utility to the Consumer Organizations, individual consumers as well as to the legal profession. Though this pioneer work has filled a void in the legal literature relating to consumer protection, it does not deal with the concept of consumer awareness as such.

J.N. Barowalia (1996), in his book "*Commentary on Consumer Protection Act, 1986*" has explained each and every provisions of the Act in detail and incorporated in rules framed by the Central Government and the State Governments from time to time. The laws laid down by the Supreme Court, National Commission and state consumer have been incorporated at the appropriate places in the book, and it is a very comprehensive commentary on the Consumer Protection Act.

P.K. Mujumdar (1997), in his book "*Law of Consumer Protection in India*" has referred to a large number of rulings of the Supreme Court, the High Courts, the National Commission and the State Commissions. It is a practical guide to the District Forums, Bench and Bar, Chartered Accountants, Company Secretaries, various Consumer Organisations, Government Offices, students and public at large. It contains an extensive coverage of case laws from various Journals published in India on consumer disputes viz., Consumer Protection Reporter, Consumer Protection Journal,

Consumer Protection Cases, Consumer Protection and Trade Practices Journal etc.

B.K. Das and S.S. Rao (1999), have authored a book on consumer protection. This book "*A Commentary on Consumer Protection Act, 1986*" covers the relevant Central and State Consumer Protection Rules for knocking the doors of consumer redressal agencies.

Sukhdev Aggarwal's (2003) book "*Commentary on the Consumer Protection Act, 1986*" containing comprehensive information on all topics of the Consumer Protection Act becomes helpful not only to the members of the legal profession, but also to the general public and the voluntary consumer organizations'.

O.P. Garg's book "*The Consumer Protection Act, 1986*" deals with the subject of consumer protection in a historical retrospect and shows stage by stage the development of laws relating to consumer movement in the country. The book is quite helpful to both the consumers and the producers.

Suresh Patidar (2008), concluded that consumer awareness is very important to protect the interest of the consumers. The study has tried to reveal the fact that how much deep rooted is the problem of consumer awareness. The awareness among the consumers can be increased by sincere efforts of government and also to some extent by society.

A.K. Chandra (2011), observed that "*The Consumer Protection Act, 1986*", is one of the socio-economic legislation, which has been enacted for protecting the interests of the consumers in India. Unlike existing laws, which are punitive or preventive in nature, the provisions of this Act are compensatory in nature. The Act is also intended to provide simple, speedy and inexpensive redressal to the consumers' grievances, and relief of a specific nature and award of compensation, wherever appropriate, to the consumer.

Research Methodology

The present study is aimed at analysing the role and performance of the National Consumer Disputes Redressal Commission in the growth and consolidation of the consumer protection movement in India. For the purpose of the study, data has been collected and analyzed with the help of secondary data from various sources like books, articles, referred journal and website.

Development of the Consumer Protection Law and Policy in India

The Consumer Protection Act, 1986 was hailed as a milestone in the history of socio-economic legislation in our country. Under this Act any buyer or consumer of goods or services is entitled to seek remedy against the seller for defective goods or services or deficient quality of goods or services supply.

The Monopolies and Restrictive Trade Practices Act, 1969 (now repealed) was enacted to prevent the concentration of economic power to the common detriment and to prohibit monopolistic and restrictive trade practices which were prejudicial to the public interest. In the year 1984, the provision relating to the Act by virtue of enactment of the Monopolies and Restrictive Trade Practices (Amendment) Act, 1984. This Act was aimed at keeping watch on big businesses and to safeguard the interests of consumers. The provisions of this Act cover 'goods' as well as 'services'. The goods are those which are manufactured or produced and sold to consumers through wholesalers and retailers. The services are in the nature of transport, telephone, electricity, housing, banking, insurance, medical treatment etc. A written complaint, can be filed before the District Consumer Forum for pecuniary value of upto Rupees twenty lakh, State Commission for value up to Rupees one crore and the National Commission for value above Rupees one crore, in respect of defects in goods and or deficiency in service. The service can be of any description and the illustrations given above are only indicative. However, no complaint can be filed for alleged deficiency in any service that is rendered free of charge or under a contract of personal service.

The National Consumer Disputes Redressal Commission (NCDRC) is at the apex. The National Consumer Disputes

Redressal Commission is a quasi-judicial commission which was set up in 1988 under the Consumer Protection Act of 1986. The National Consumer Disputes Redressal Commission (NCDRC), India is a quasi-judicial commission in India which was set up in 1988 under the Consumer Protection Act of 1986. Its head office is in New Delhi. The commission is headed by a sitting or retired judge of the Supreme Court of India. The commission is presently headed by Justice D.K. Jain, former judge of the Supreme Court of India.

Section 21 of the Consumer Protection Act, 1986 posits that the National Consumer shall have jurisdiction to entertain a complaint valued more than one crore and also have Appellate and Revisional jurisdiction from the orders of State Commissions or the District fora as the case may be. Section 23 of Consumer Protection Act, 1986, provides that any person aggrieved by an order of NCDRC, may prefer an Appeal against such order to Supreme Court of India within a period of 30 days.

The Consumer Protection Act, 1986 (In short, 'The Act') is a benevolent social legislation that lays down the rights of the consumers and provides for promotion and protection of the rights of the consumers. The first and the only Act of its kind in India, it has enabled ordinary consumers to secure less expensive and often speedy redressal of their grievances. By spelling out the rights and remedies of the consumers in a market so far dominated by organized manufacturers and traders of goods and providers of various types of services, the Act makes the dictum, caveat emptor ('Buyer Beware') a thing of the past. The Act mandates establishment of Consumer Protection Councils at the Centre as well as in each State and District, with a view to promoting consumer awareness. The Central Council is headed by Minster In-charge of the Department of Consumer Affairs in the Central Government and the State Councils by the Minister In-charge of the Consumer Affairs in the State Governments. It also provides for a 3-tier structure of the National and State Commissions and District Forums for speedy resolution of consumer disputes.

According to section 9, for the purposes of the Consumer Protection Act, 1986, three types of Consumer Disputes Redressal Agencies shall be established. These three agencies are as follows:

1. Consumer Disputes Redressal Forum—Also known as District Consumer Forum.
2. Consumer Disputes Redressal Commission—Also known as the State Commission.
3. National Consumer Disputes Redressal Commission—Also known as the National Commission.

To provide inexpensive, speedy and summary redressal of consumer disputes, quasi-judicial bodies have been set up in each District and State and at the National level, called the District Forums, the State Consumer Disputes Redressal Commissions and the National Consumer Disputes Redressal Commission respectively. At present, there are 629 District Forums and 35 State Commissions with the National Consumer Disputes Redressal Commission (NCDRC) at the apex. NCDRC has its office at Upbhokta Nyay Bhawan, 'F' Block, GPO Complex, INA, New Delhi-110 023. The remedy under the Consumer Protection Act is an alternative in addition to that already available to the aggrieved persons/consumers by way of civil suit. In the complaint/appeal/ petition submitted under the Act, a consumer is not required to pay any court fees but only a nominal fee.

Each District Forum is headed by a person who is or has been or is eligible to be appointed as a District Judge and each State Commission is headed by a person who is or has been a Judge of High Court. The National Commission was constituted in the year 1988. It is headed by a sitting or retired Judge of the Supreme Court of India. Apart from the President it also has judicial and non-judicial members.

Consumer Fora proceedings are summary in nature. The endeavour is made to grant relief to the aggrieved consumer as quickly as in the quickest possible, keeping in mind the provisions of the Act which lay down time schedule for disposal of cases. If a consumer is not satisfied by the decision of a District Forum, he can appeal to the State Commission. Against the order of the State Commission a consumer can come to the National Commission. In order to help achieve the objects of the Consumer Protection Act, the National Commission has also been conferred with the powers of administrative control over all the State Commissions by calling for periodical returns regarding the institution, disposal and pendency of cases. The National Commission is empowered to issue instructions regarding:

1. Adoption of uniform procedure in the hearing of the matters,
2. Prior service of copies of documents produced by one party to the opposite parties,
3. Speedy grant of copies of documents, and
4. Generally over-seeing the functioning of the State Commissions and the District Fora to ensure that the objects and purposes of the Act are best served, without interfering with their quasi-judicial freedom.

The Registry of the National Commission is at the Ground Floor, Upbhokta Nyay Bhawan, 'F' Block, GPO Complex, INA, New Delhi-110 023 which remains open on all working days. For any enquiry with the Registry of the National Commission, one can contact on Telephone Nos. 011-24608801, 24608802, 24608803, 24608804 and Fax No. 24651505. The filing timings are from 10.00 a.m. to 4.30 p.m. Every matter filed with the Registry is listed on the 7th day of its filing for admission before the National Commission. Functioning of District Forum, State Commission and National Commission is consumer friendly, and thus a consumer can file a complaint and also address arguments in person. In genuine cases where the complainant/appellant/petitioner before the National Commission is unable to engage the services of an advocate legal aid is provided by the Commission free of charge.

Details under Right to Information Act, 2005

The National Commission has considered the points mentioned under Section 4 of the Right of Information Act, 2005 and its Observations on the said points are given below:

Sl. No.	Points	Comments
(i)	The particulars of its organization functions and duties.	The National Consumer Disputes Redressal Commission has been set up under Consumer Protection Act, 1986 for better protection of interest of the Consumers. It is a quasi-judicial body consisting of President and 11 Members. The Commission has three types of jurisdiction, i.e. Original, Appellate and Revisional. It has been receiving complaints, Appeals and Revision Petitions from the consumers from all over the country. The National Commissions has been functioning as per the provisions laid down in the Consumer Protection Act, 1986.
(ii)	The Powers and duties of its officers and employees.	Being a quasi-judicial body, the nature of work in the Commission is different from other Government Departments. Even the Central Government or any State Government can file a Complaint in the Consumer Forums as they are covered by the definition of "Complainant" as defined in Section 2(b) (iii) of the Act. The Complaints Appeals and Revision Petitions are being received and processed under the supervision of the Registrar by the officers and staff members of the National Commission for placing the same before Hon'ble Benches for hearing. Besides, the staff posted in Administration Section is looking after the administrative work of the National Commission.

(*Contd.*)

Sl. No.	Points	Comments
		Section 24-B—The National Commission shall have administrative control over all the State Commissions in the matters enumerated under Section 24-B of the Consumer Protection Act, 1986.
(iii)	The procedure followed in the decision making process, including channels of supervision and accountability.	The National Commission is a quasi-judicial body and all the decisions in Consumer Complaints/Appeals and Revision Petitions are taken by the Hon'ble Benches, constituted by the Hon'ble President with one or more Members as the President may deem fit and are being decided as per the provisions of the Consumer Protection Act, 1986. Under Section 23 of the Act, a consumer can file an Appeal before the Hon'ble Supreme Court of India against the decision of the National Commission. As regards the administrative matters the President of the Commission has been declared the 'Head of the Department'.
(iv)	The norms set by it for the discharge of its functions.	The Central Government has notified Consumer Protection Rules, 1987 as well as Regulations, 2005 providing therein the norms for filing of cases. Accordingly, Commission is discharging its quasi-judicial functions within the purview of the said Rules & Regulations. The officers and other employees are governed by the service rules applicable to Central Government employees.
(v)	The rules, regulations, instructions, manuals and records held by its employees for discharging its functions.	As regards Rules & Regulations, the Central Government has already notified Consumer Protection Rules, 1987 and the National Commission has notified the Regulations with prior consent of the Central Government under Section 30A of Consumer Protection Act, 1986. They are public documents and can be accessed from the website of the Commission.

(*Contd.*)

Sl. No.	Points	Comments
(vi)	A statement of the categories of documents that are held by it or under its control.	As regards categories of documents that are held by the Commission, it is stated that the Commission has been receiving complaints, Appeals and Revision Petitions from consumers and they are the main documents in the forms of cases under its control.
(vii)	The particulars of any arrangement that exist for consultation with, or representation by the members of the public in relation to the formulation of its policy or implementation thereof.	Not Applicable.
(viii)	A statement of the boards, councils, committees and other bodies consisting of two or more persons constituted as its part or for the purpose of its advice, and as to whether meetings of those boards, councils, committees and other bodies are open to the public, or the minutes of such meetings are accessible for public.	Not Applicable.

(*Contd.*)

Sl. No.	Points	Comments
(ix)	A directory of its officers and employees.	Directory containing the addresses and telephone numbers of NCDRC, State Commissions and District Forums spread all over the country including their officers and an employee has already been placed on the website of the National Commission, i.e. www.ncdrc.nic.in.
(x)	The monthly remuneration received by each of its officers and employees, including the system of compensation as provided in its regulations.	All the officers and employees of the Commission are in receipt of the monthly pay and allowances as are applicable to the Central Government officers and employees.
(xi)	The budget allocated to each of its agency, indicating the particulars of all plans, proposed expenditures and reports on disbursements made.	Department of Consumer Affairs is allocating the budget to the National Commission and the same is available in the Demands for Grants of the Department of Consumer Affairs, Government of India.
(xii)	The manner of execution of subsidy programmes, including the amounts allocated and the details of beneficiaries of such programmes.	Not Applicable.

(*Contd.*)

Sl. No.	Points	Comments
(xiii)	Particulars of recipients of concessions, permits of authorizations granted by it.	Not Applicable.
(xiv)	Details in respect of the information, available to or held by it, reduced in an electronic form.	The relevant information of the Consumer Protection Act, Rules, Regulations, general information regarding listing of cases and important orders passed by the National Commission are available on its website, i.e. www.ncdrc.nic.in.
(xv)	The particulars of facilities available to citizens for obtaining information, including the working hours of a library or reading room, if maintained for public use.	The National Commission launched its website, i.e. www.ncdrc.nic.in in the year 2002 and the following information is available on its website: (a) Consumer Protection Act, 1986 (b) Consumer Protection Rules, 1987 (c) Consumer Protection Regulations, 2005 (d) General information (e) Procedure for filing of cases before National Commission (f) Statistics regarding filing, disposal and pendency of cases (g) Calendar of sittings (h) Notices (i) Link sites—Department of Consumer Affairs (Supreme Court/High Courts). (j) Addresses of State Commissions and District Forums etc. (k) Important orders of the NCDRC. As regards the Library or reading room is concerned, due to shortage of office space the Commission is not in a position to set up a separate library for public. However, a small library has already been set up by the Commission for the Hon'ble President, Members and its staff.

(*Contd.*)

Sl. No.	Points	Comments
(xvi)	The names, designations and other particulars of the Public Information Officers.	The names and designations of the Appellate Authority and CPIOs appointed under Right to Information Act, 2005 are as under: 1. Mr. S.H. Rao—Appellate Authority, Joint Registrar 2. Mr. Iqbal Ahmed—Nodal CPIO Deputy Registrar 3. Mr. H.C. Joshi—CPIO (RP) Assistant Registrar 4. Mr. S. Viswanathan—CPIO (FA) Assistant Registrar 5. Mr. Dalip Lamba—CPIO (CC) Court Master (NS) 6. Mr. Rajesh Nath—Estt. Section Assistant Registrar 7. Mr. R.M. Naidu—CPIO Accounts Officer (Accounts) 8. Mr. L.N. Arora—CPIO Section Officer (Gen. Admin.) 9. Mr. Yatinder Kr. Sakkarwal—ACPIO UDC
(xvii)	Such other information as may be prescribed; thereafter update these publications every year.	—

Source: ncdrc.nic.in/

As per the Consumer Protection Act, 1986 a complaint can be filed in:

District Consumer Disputes Redressal Forum (DCDRF): If the value of the claim is up to Rs. 20 lakh. State Consumer Disputes Redressal Commission (SCDRC): If the value of the claim exceeds Rs. 20 lakhs but is within Rs. 1 crore. National Consumer Disputes Redressal Commission (NCDRC) if the value of the claim exceeds rupees one crore.

Structure for Redressal Mechanism

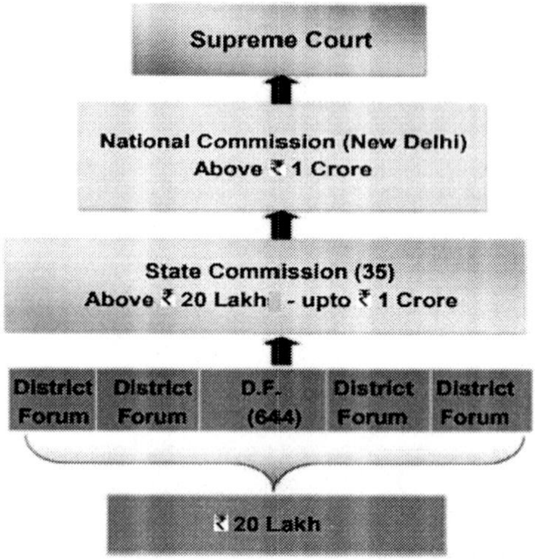

As per the Consumer Protection Act, 1986 a complaint can be filed in:

District Consumer Disputes Redressal Forum (DCDRF): If the value of the claim is up to Rs. 20 lakh. State Consumer Disputes Redressal Commission (SCDRC): If the value of the claim exceeds Rs. 20 lakh but is within Rs. 1 crore. National Consumer Disputes Redressal Commission (NCDRC) if the value of the claim exceeds Rs. 1 crore.

Is there any Fee for filing Complaint ?

Every complaint filed shall be accompanied by a fee as specified in the Table given below in the form of crossed Demand Draft drawn on a nationalized bank or through across Indian Postal Order drawn in favour of the Registrar of the State Commission and payable at the respective place where the State Commission or the National Commission is situated.

Sl. No.	Total Value of goods or services and the compensation claimed (in₹)	Amount of fee payable (in₹)
	District Forum	
(1)	Up to one lakh rupees – For complainants who are Below Poverty Line holding Antyodaya Anna Yojana Cards	Nil
(2)	Up to one lakh rupees – For complainants other than Antyodaya Anna Yojana card holders.	100
(3)	Above one lakh and up to five lakh rupees	200
(4)	Above five lakh and up to ten lakh rupees	400
(5)	Above ten lakh and up to twenty lakh rupees	500
	State Commission	
(6)	Above twenty lakh and up to fifty lakh rupees	2000
(7)	Above fifty lakh and up to one crore rupees	4000
	National Commission	
(8)	Above one crore rupees	5000

What is the Jurisdiction of Consumer Fora ?

A complaint shall be instituted in a Consumer Forum within the local limits of whose jurisdiction the opposite party resides or carries on business or has a branch office or personally works for gain, or where the cause of action, wholly or in part, arises.

Is there any exemption from payment of Fee ?

The complainants who are Below the Poverty Line shall be entitled for the exemption of payment of fee for complaints up to rupees one lakh on production of an attested copy of the Antyodaya Anna Yojana Card.

How to file a Complaint ?

1. The complaint can be filed on a plain paper.
2. Stamp paper is not required for declaration.
3. It should contain the details of the complainant and the opposite party.
4. Complaint can be registered, in person, by the complainant or through his authorized agent or by post addressed to the Redressal Agency.

5. It is not compulsory to engage a lawyer to file a case.
6. The fees charged are very nominal according to the value of the claim.

What are the Particulars that Should be Furnished along with the Complaint ?

The complaint should contain the following particulars:

1. Name and complete address of the complainant.
2. Name and complete address of the opposite party/parties.
3. Date of purchase of goods or services availed.
4. Amount paid for the above purpose.
5. Particulars of goods purchased with numbers or details of services availed.
6. Details of complaint, whether it is against Unfair Trade Practice/supply of defective goods/deficiency in service provided/collection of excess price should explicitly be mentioned in the complaint petition.
7. Bills/receipts and copies of connected correspondence, if any.
8. Relief sought for under this Act.
9. Complaint should be signed by the complainant or his authorised agent.

What is the Provision for Appeal ?

1. Aggrieved by the Order issued by the District Forum, appeal petition may be filed before the State Commission within 30 days from the date of receipt of Order.
2. Aggrieved by the Order issued by the State Commission, appeal petition may be filed before the National Commission within 30 days from the date of receipt of Order.
3. Aggrieved by the Order issued by the National Commission, appeal petition may be filed before the Supreme Court of India within 30 days from the date of receipt of Orders.

Conclusion and Suggestions

The Consumer Protection Act was enacted by Parliament in 1986. This Act created Consumer Councils and other forums to settle the consumer disputes. This Act seeks to promote and protect rights of consumers, such as: (I) The right to be protected against marketing of goods which are hazardous to life and property; (2) The right to be informed about the quality, quantity, potency, purity, standard and price of the goods to protect consumer against unfair trade practice; (3) Right to be assured that consumer interest will receive due consideration at appropriate authority; (4) The right to be assured access to a variety of goods at competitive price; (5) The right to seek redressal against unfair trade practice or unscrupulous exploitation of consumers; and (6) Right to consumer education.

Consumer protection is always a matter of great concern. From the analysis of performance with regard to the disposal rate of cases of various Consumer Disputes Redressal Agencies in India, it is found that the agencies at the district level are on the top followed by national level and state level it is observed that district level agencies are working more efficiently than the national and state level agencies. There is still need of agencies functioning at state and national level to dispose of the pending cases as early as possible by creating supplementary benches as per the provisions of Consumer Protection Act, 1986.

Note

1. Department of Consumer Studies, Government of India and the Centre for Consumer Studies, Indian Institute of Public Administration, New Delhi, 2011, p. 11.

References

Barowalia, J.N. (1996). *Commentary on the Consumer Protection Act, 1986*, Delhi: Universal Law Publishing Co., p. 3.

Bhatnagar, Subir K. (1991). "A Blue Print of Trident Strategy for Consumer Protection in India", *Law Journal M.D.U.*, Vol. 2, Dec., p. 7.

Chaudhary, H.C. (1982). "Consumer Protection in India", *Indian Journal of Marketing*, Vol. XIII, Sept.-Oct., pp. 15-16.

Eradi Balkrishan V. (1991). "Consumer Protection: Legislation and Awareness in India", *Law Journal M.D.U.*, pp. 1-6.

Garg, O.P. (1992). *The Consumer Protection Act, 1986,* Delhi: Vinod Publishing House.

Khamesra, Vijendra B. (1980). "Consumer Protection in India," *Indian Journal of Marketing*, Vol. IX, Nov., pp. 15-18.

Majumdar, P.K. (1997). *Law Consumer Protection in India*, New Delhi: Orient Publishing Company.

Patidar Suresh (2013). "The Consumer Protection Act, 1986 of India-25 Years of Enactment: A Critical Study", *Pacific Business Review International,* Vol. 6, Issue 6, December.

Sahu, G.N. (1981). "Consumer Problems in India," *Indian Journal of Marketing*, Vol. XI, May, pp. 3-8.

Saxena, A.K. (1978). "Consumerism, Consumer Co-operative and Consumer Unity," *Indian Journal of Marketing*, Vol. IX, Dec., pp. 3-7.

Singh, Gurbax (1993). *Law of Consumer Protection*, Jaipur: Bharat Law Publications.

Singh, Kiran (1992). "Consumer Awareness," *Consumer Confrontation*, Vol. I, p. 16.

Subramanyam, D.A.R. (1982). "Need for Consumer Organization," *Indian Journal of Marketing*, Vol. 12, Oct., p. 17.

Thakur Sharmila (1992). *Product Dissonance, Consumer Opinion of Indian Marketing and Comparison of Consumer Laws of Some Country.*

Website:

https://www.lawctopus.com/academike/consumer-dispute-redrsal-agencies/

https://en.wikipedia.org/wiki/National_Consumer_Disputes_Redressal_Commission

www.drishtiias.com/upsc-exam-gs-resources-National-Consumer-Dispute-Redressal-C

Website of the Department: http://consumeraffairs.nic.in

Website of the NDRC: http://ncdrc.nic.in/ State Commisssion : http://ncdrc.nic.in/statelist.html District Forums: http://ncdrc.nic.in/districtlist.html

8

Consumption Behaviour of Liquid Milk in Imphal, East District of Manipur

Lalgoulen Khongsai, A.S. Rapheileng, Kh. Tomba Singh and *Md. Kheiruddin Shah*

Introduction

Imphal East is a home for an estimated 4,56,113 persons. The District has an area of 709 square kilometres representing 3.18 per cent of the total geographical area of the state. It is the sixth largest district in Manipur and is the biggest of the four valley districts in area (Directorate of Census Operation, 2011). The district has produced a total of 7,91,000 tonnes of milk during the year 2015-16 (Economic Survey Manipur, 2016-17, 2017). The availability of milk in the district per person during the year 2015-16 is a mere 0.067 gms per day which is much below the national and state level. The overall Per Capita Availability of Milk for the Year 2016-17 at all India level is 352 gm per day whereas Per Capita Availability of Milk for the Year 2016-17 of Manipur is 75 gm per day (Department of Animal Husbandry, 2017).

Imam, Zadeh and Dubey (2011) pointed out that though India is the world's largest milk producer it is consuming almost 100 per cent of its own milk production. Dairy products are a major source of cheap and nutritious food to millions of people in India and the only acceptable source of animal protein for large vegetarian segment of Indian population, particularly among the landless, small and marginal farmers and women.

Manipur is a store house of games and sports and milk is the most important dietary food for a sportsperson. There is a large scope of improvement in the production of milk in the study area where sports institute and Khuman Lampak main stadium is located. However, *Huiyen Lanpao* (2015), a local daily newspaper has reported a drastic drop in the production of milk in the state by citing the frequent flood, bandhs and blockades which had created transportation bottlenecks in the regular supply of cattle fodder from outside the state. They also reported that milk collectors, unscrupulous traders and suppliers have committed unfair trade practices by selling adulterated milk, unhygienic packages and milk without expiry date which can be harmful for human consumption.

The present study is undertaken with the objectives to acquire the knowledge of consumer perception and behaviour while making purchase decision. The findings will be helpful for the consumer to make the right decision while making choice of liquid milk. The descriptive statistics of the study will be helpful in knowing the socio-economic conditions of the consumer of the study area. The relationship study will throw light to obtain an in-depth knowledge about the variables under study.

Production and Consumption Pattern of Milk

Dhawan (2016) highlighted that India's milk production exceeds 258 million litres per day (94 million tonnes per annum). Some 70 million farmers maintain a milch herd of about 105 million (58 million cows and 47 million buffaloes) feeding largely on crop residues which account for 98 per cent of all milk produced in India. Dairy sector in India is important for its complementary relationship with agriculture and for its capability to provide protein rich diet to the vegetarian population. Due to the remunerative price received by the milk producer, the milk economy is transforming from a subsistence activity to commercial activity. The consumer has also benefited because the increase in milk prices has been generally lower than the rate of inflation compared to other food products.

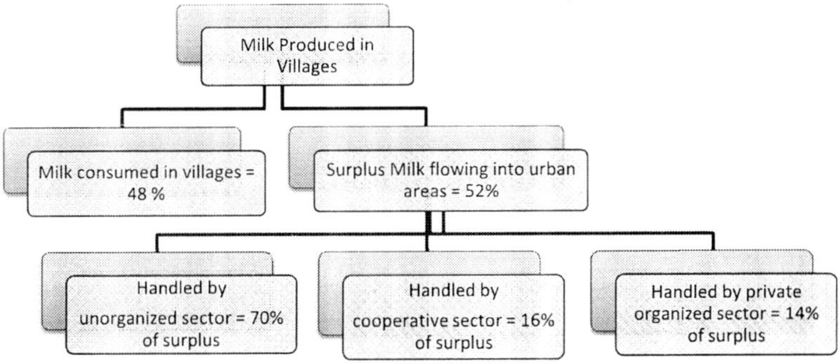

Fig. 8.1: Production, Distribution and Consumption Pattern of Milk Produced In Indian Villages

Source: National Dairy Plan 2007-08 to 2011-12, Department of Animal Husbandry, Government of India. (adopted from Chawla & Chawla, 2009).

Sachiffman and Kanuk (2008; as cited in Elangovan & Gomatheeswaran, 2015) defined consumer behaviour as the behaviour that consumers display in searching for, purchasing, using, evaluating and disposing of products and services that they expect will satisfy their needs and wants. They elaborated further, by stating that consumer behaviour focuses on how individuals make decisions to spend their available resources (time, money, effort) on consumption related items. That includes what, why, when, where they buy? How often they buy and use it? How they evaluate it after the purchase and its impact on future purchases? and how they dispose of it? They concluded by saying that consumer buying decision process start much before the products have been acquired or bought.

Table 8.1: Year-wise milk production (000' tonnes)

Year	All India	Manipur (%)	Year	All India	Manipur (%)
2002-03	86159	69(0.08)	2009-10	116425	78(0.07)
2003-04	88082	71(0.08)	2010-11	121848	78(0.06)
2004-05	92484	75(0.08)	2011-12	127904	79(0.06)
2005-06	97066	77(0.08)	2012-13	132431	80(0.06)
2006-07	102580	77(0.08)	2013-14	137685	82(0.06)
2007-08	107934	78(0.07)	2014-15	146314	82(0.06)
2008-09	112183	78(0.07)	2015-16	155491	79(0.05)

Source: Department of Animal Husbandry, Dairying & Fisheries, Ministry of Agriculture, GoI.

Table 8.1 shows the average milk production for the last 14 years at the national and Manipur. From the Table it is understood that the average production of milk at the national level is 116041.85 thousand tonnes (min=86159 and max=155491.00) whereas Manipur produce milk on an average of 77.35 thousand tonnes with a maximum of 82.00 and a minimum of 69.00 thousand tonnes in the last 14 years.

Table 8.2: Year-wise Per Capita Milk Availability (gms/day)

Year	All India	Manipur (%)	Year	All India	Manipur (%)
2002-03	230	85	2009-10	273	88
2003-04	231	85	2010-11	281	88
2004-05	233	90	2011-12	290	80
2005-06	241	92	2012-13	299	80
2006-07	251	91	2013-14	307	80

(*Contd.*)

Year	All India	Manipur (%)	Year	All India	Manipur (%)
2007-08	260	91	2014-15	322	80
2008-09	266	90	2015-16	337	76

Source: Department of Animal Husbandry, Dairying & Fisheries, Ministry of Agriculture, GoI.

Literature Review

Barad and Mehta (2017) in their study on consumer preference towards packed and unpacked milk in Veraval city suggested that the consumer always considered different factors like the standard quality of milk, fat level, price, freshness and availability before making a purchase. They concluded that these are the various variables which guide or direct the consumer to make the purchase decision.

Naami, developed a dynamic model to evaluate the factors affecting the ice cream promotion methods and its brands. They found that key characteristics of the product such as having standard, taste, brand reputation, quality, type of packaging etc. are the characteristics that have the greatest impact on consumer behaviour and they are very effective to make decision and adopt strategies for marketing ice cream.

Trung *et al.* (2014) had applied two-step econometric technique to measure the effects of the socio-economic and demographic factors and characteristics of milk market on milk consumption of the rural households and they found that household's income and convenience in milk buying has strong positive effects on milk consumption. At the lighter level, numbers of children and elders also had positive effects on the probability of milk both purchasing and milk expenditure whereas educational level was found to affect milk expenditure only. In contrast, age of the rural household head and the importance of milk and its price had significant negative effects on both decisions of milk consumption and level of milk expenditure.

Papaioannou, Tzimitra-Kalogianni, and Tegkelidou (2015) concluded that the consumers mainly purchase fresh milk from the super market. Brand of the fresh milk, the taste, the nutritional ingredients, the quality, the location, the packaging, the price, and discounts are factors responsible for purchasing decision. They found that brands and advertisement as the main factor for the purchase decision. They also found that televisions were the main mass media for fresh milk, followed by the internet, magazines, and newspapers. They suggested that advertisement should include the information on safety of fresh milk.

Haghighat and Niavand (2015) according to statistics available per capita consumption of this nutrient among Indians is well below the world average that this rate of prevalence of diseases such as osteoporosis, calcium deficiency and many other diseases among Indians enhances the frequency of losses and losses for the country. Though very heavy losses and calculate an integral charges physical and mental growth can be accounted for essentially not. Due to this short introduction to the need for extensive research in order to check the effects of various factors on consumer behaviour mechanism dairy products is inevitable. In line with this study it was felt necessary to do. This research attempts to answer this question is the impact of marketing milk factors (income, familiarity with various types of dairy products, easy access to milk, packaging and the importance of awareness of the benefits of milk in their study on the analysis of marketing milk factories and effects on customers behaviour mechanism revealed that income, familiarity with various types of dairy products, easy access to milk, packaging and the importance and awareness of the benefits of milk were the main factors in the marketing and consumption of dairy products.

Objectives of the Study

1. To study milk production and consumption pattern at the national level and Manipur state.
2. To examine the socio-economic characteristics of the consumers and its impact on liquid milk consumption.

3. To identify the factors influencing consumers' buying decision on liquid milk.

Hypothesis

Ho1: Size of the family and total family income does not have significant relationship on the average daily consumption of liquid milk.
Ho2: The average consumption level of liquid milk in Manipur does not differ with the average consumption level of liquid milk in the national level.

Research Methodology

Samples

The study was conducted in Imphal East District of Manipur which is a composition of different communities, namely Meitei, Meitei Pangal, Kuki, Nagas and others (minor communities like Nepali, Biharis and Marwaris etc.). Considering the different communities which comprised the population of the study area the researchers took due care to include respondents from each community. Thus a total of 105 respondents representing the various communities were selected through random sampling and interviewed by using a structured interview schedule.

Materials

Both primary and secondary data were used for the study. Primary data was collected through the way of direct conversation with the consumer by using questionnaire method. Whereas Secondary data was collected from various publications, journals, magazines, articles from newspaper, publications from state and Central Government departments, research articles available on various websites and other internet sources. The data were collected during the month of April 2017 to August 2017.

Analysis

The data gathered were codified and then administered using SPSS

English version 21.0 for analyses. Statistical tools like descriptive statistics, independent t-test and correlation were used for the analyses of research data.

Table 8.3: Socio-Economic Profile of the Respondents

Variables	Group	n= 105 (%)
Gender	Male	69 (65.7%)
	Female	36 (34.3%)
Marital Status	Unmarried	30 (28.6%)
	Married	70 (66.7%)
	Divorced	5 (4.8%)
Educational Qualification	Below 10th	42 (40%)
	10 + 2	32 (30.5%)
	Graduate	19 (18.1%)
	Postgraduate	10 (9.5%)
	Any other	2 (1.9%)
Occupation	Govt. employee	23 (21.9%)
	Business	46 (43.8%)
	Professional	3 (2.9%)
	Any other	33 (31.4%)
Religion	Christianity	45 (42.9%)
	Hinduism	33(31.4%)
	Islam	23 (21.9%)
	Others	4 (3.8%)
Social Status	ST	51 (48.6%)
	OBC	35 (33.3%)
	General	19 (18.1%)
Types of family	Joint	40 (40%)
	Extended	14 (13.3%)
	Nuclear	49 (46.7%)

Source: Computed from Primary data.

Table 8.3 exhibits the socio-economic profile of the respondents. Out of the total 105 respondents, male comprised 69 (65.7%) and female comprised 36 (34.5%) of which 70 (66.7%) were married. Educational qualification showed that more than one-fourth of the respondents numbering 42 (40%) possessed educational level which is below 10th standard. 46 (43.8%) of the respondents are engaged in business. Highest numbers of respondents are Christian comprising 45 (42.9%). Nearly Half of the respondents 51 (48.6%) are under the ambit of Scheduled Tribe. Out of the total respondents nuclear type of family is the maximum with 49 (46.7%) of the family belonging to this structure.

Table 8.4: Factors Influencing Liquid Milk Consumption

Variables	Group	n= 105 (%)
Consumption Motivation	Lifestyle	3 (2.9%)
	Health consciousness	83 (79%)
	Taste	17 (16.2%)
	Influence by family/friends	2 (1.9%)
Purchase Motivation	Taste	20 (19%)
	Price	4 (3.8%)
	Easy availability	16 (15.2%)
	Home delivery	46 (43.8%)
	Any other	19 (18.1%)
Preference types	Package pasteurized milk	48 (45.7%)
	Un pack local fresh milk	57 (54.3%)
Packaging preference	Colour	7 (6.7%)
	Design	7 (6.7%)
	Brand	25 (23.8%)
	Size	22 (21%)
	Loose pack	44 (41.9%)

Source: Computed from Primary data.

Table 8.4 presents the factors influencing consumption of liquid milk. Maximum of the respondents 83 (79%) were motivated to consume milk due to health consciousness. Regarding reasons for purchase decision, 46 (43.8%) respondents rated home delivery as the most important followed by taste (19%). As with package preference, more than half 57 (54.3%) preferred unpacked local fresh milk whereas the others 48 (45.7%) preferred packed pasteurized milk. Colour and design of package did not have much influence on purchase of liquid milk.

Table 8.5: Consumption Pattern of liquid milk

Variables	Group	n= 105 (%)
Consumption Pattern	Once daily	64 (61%)
	Twice daily	36 (34.3%)
	Thrice daily	4 (3.8%)
	More than thrice daily	1 (1%)
Amount spent	Less than Rs.300	8 (7.6%)
	Rs. 300-600	23 (21.9%)
	Rs. 600-900	24 (22.9%)
	Rs. 900-1200	24 (22.9%)
	Rs. 1200 and above	26 (24.8%)
Purchase Point	Dairy farm	4 (3.8%)
	Shop	30 (28.6%)
	Milk booth	9 (8.6%)
	Home delivery	61 (58.1%)
	Own Production	1 (1%)

Source: Computed from Primary data.

Table 8.5 displayed the consumption pattern of liquid milk. The frequency of milk consumption was very low on average as more than half of the consumer 64 (61%) consumed milk only once daily. Out of the total consumers, 71 (67.61%) on an average spend Rs. 300 to Rs. 1200 monthly. Regarding purchase point,

61(58.1%) of the respondents consider home delivery as the best option which is followed by shop 30 (28.6%).

Table 8.6: Mean Standard Deviation, Minimum and Maximum of the control variables and output variables

Variables	Mean	Standard Deviation	Minimum	Maximum
Size of the family	5.40	2.29	1.0	12.0
Income (in Rs.)	29766.66	27719.49	1000	150000
Consumption of milk (in litres)	1.31	0.65	0.50	5.0

Source: Computed from Primary data.

Table 8.6 highlighted the descriptive statistics of the respondents. The minimum size of the family is 1 while the maximum is 12 with mean size of 5.40 (SD ± 2.29). The average monthly income of the respondent family was Rs. 29,766.66 with a minimum of Rs. 1000 and maximum of Rs. 1,50,000. The average consumption of fresh milk is 1.31 litres per day with a minimum of 0.50 litres and a maximum of 5 litres.

Table 8.7: Correlation Analysis of Income and Size of the Family with Consumption

(n=105)

Variables	Income	Size of the family
Pearson correlation	0.025	0.156
Consumption sig. (2-tailed)	0.803	0.111

Source: Computed from Primary data.

Correlation analyses were used to examine the relationship between size as well as income of the family with that of the amount of milk consumption. The result indicated that the consumption of liquid milk did not have any significant relationship with size of the family ($r = 0.156$, $p = 0.111$) and income ($r = 0.025$, $p = 0.803$).

Table 8.8: Mean, SD and T-test of the Per Capita Milk Availability

National		Manipur		t	p-value
Mean	**SD**	**Mean**	**SD**	**20.00**	**0.000**
272.92	34.66	85.42	5.31		

Source: Computed from Table 8.2.

Table 8.8 presented the result of t-test of year wise per capita availability of liquid milk between all India level and Manipur state. The result revealed that there was significant difference (t=20.005, p=0.000) in the consumption level of milk between all India level and Manipur, meaning which the null hypothesis (Ho2) was rejected (at 5% significant level). Explaining that the per capita milk availability at the national level (M=272.92, SD=34.66) was significantly higher than that of Manipur (M=85.43, SD= 5.31).

Discussion and Conclusion

This study investigated the consumer behaviour and factors influencing the consumption of liquid milk in Imphal East. Though milk economically is cheap and nutritious, the per capita consumption of the state is very low with only 75 gm per person per day whereas it was 352 gm per day at the national level during the year under study. There was a huge gap of differences in the average consumption of milk at the state and the national level. It was found that the production of milk in the state was deficit even for own consumption. This is in congruent with the study by Imam, Zadeh and Dubey (2011), where they pointed out that India consumed 100 per cent of its production. Regarding familial liquid milk consumption level size and income of the family were independent of consumption contradicting with the findings of Trung *et al.,* (2014), where household's income had strong positive impact on milk consumption.

Some limitations were found in the collection and interpretation of the data. Although the sample size was deemed acceptable, a larger sample would have allowed us to run more analyses.

Question on the preference type of milk like skimmed, toned and pasteurized could have been included in the questionnaire as additional information.

The current study was limited to three aspects only that is, the study on socio-economic, factors influencing purchase decision and relationship between various factors on amount of liquid milk consumption. Future works can examine other characteristic like age-wise milk consumption, how milk is consumed (with tea or other beverages) and varieties of milk (like cow milk, buffalo milk or goat milk). Further it is a well-known fact that no two individuals have the same attitudes, personality and traits hence difference in their motivation factors. Some people are motivated by only one factor there is whereas some are motivated by more than one factors, thus, future researchers could address and improve their study by employing a larger items scale.

References

Barad, B.D. & Mehta, P. L. (2017). A study on consumer's preference towards packed and unpacked fluid milk with special reference to Veraval city. *International Journal of Marketing & Financial Management, 5*(1) 12-19. doi:org/10.5281/zenodo.238846

Chawla, A., Chawla, N., Pant,Y., & Kandhari, P. (2009). *Milk and Dairy Products in India-Production, Consumption and Exports* (Second Edition). Hindustan Studies & Services Ltd and Infolitics.

Department of Animal Husbandry (2017). *Annual Report 2016-2017.* New Delhi: Ministry of Agriculture and Farmers Welfare. Retrieved from http://dahd.nic.in/sites/default/filess/Annual%20Report%202016-17.pdf

Dhawan, S. (2016). A study of consumer behaviour towards various branded and non-branded milk with special reference to Jabalpur District in Madhya Pradesh. *Imperial Journal of Interdisciplinary Research* (*IJIR*), 2(12), 1582–1586.

Directorate of Census Operation, Government of Manipur. (2011). *District Census Handbook 2011.* Directorate of Census Operation. Retrieved from http://www.censusindia.gov.in/2011census/dchb/1407_PART_B_DCHB_IMPHAL EAST.pdf

Elangovan. N. & Gomatheeswaran, M. (2015). A study on consumer behaviour towards various brands of milk and milk products with special reference to Thudiyalur town at Coimbatore district in Tamil Nadu. *International Journal of Multidisciplinary Research and Development,* 2(4), 595-601.

Haghighat, F. R.T. & Niavand, H. (2015). The Analysis of Marketing Milk Factories and Effects on Customers Behaviours Mechanism. *Journal of Accounting & Marketing,* 4(3), 1-4. http://doi.org/10.4172/2168-9601.1000143

Huyen Lanpao. (2015, October 5). *Milk, dairy production rate drops in Manipur. Huiyen Lanpao.* Imphal. Retrieved from http://e-pao.net/GP.asp?src=20..051015.oct15

Imam, A., Zadeh, M.N. & Rani, L.D. (2011). Dairy Marketing Strategies in the Context of Globalization: Issues and Challenges: *International Journal of Trade, Economics and Finance,* 2(2), 138-144.

Naami, A., Hosseinabadi, D.S., Taheri, M. & Samadhi, M. (2015). Dynamics analysis of consumer behaviour. *International Journal of Economics, Commerce and Management,* III(2), 1-13.

Papaioannou, I., Tzimitra-Kalogianni, I. & Tegkelidou, E. (2015). The influence of advertisement in fresh milk consumers' behaviour. *CEUR Workshop Proceedings,* 1498, 573-82.

Trung, T.Q., Giam, D.Q., Hai, V.T., Thao, L.P., Thi, N., Hang, T., Linh, M. (2014). Factors Influencing Milk Consumption of Rural Households in Northern Vietnam. *Green Journal of Business and Management Studies,* 4(2), 031-040.

9

Role of Educational Institutions in Consumer Protection in Manipur

G.P. Prasain, Lalhriatchhungi and *Kiirii Onand Monsang*

Introduction

Consumer movements have marked 15th March of every year as World Consumer Rights Day since 1983.Consumers play a vital role in the development of a nation. Gandhiji in the light of the above rightly said "A customer is the most important visitor on our premises. He is not dependent on us. We are dependent on him. He is not an interruption in our work—he is the purpose of it. We are not doing him a favour by serving him. He is doing us a favour by giving us the opportunity to serve him." We live in a consumer society where consumers play a vital role in the development of a nation. Developments have made a great impact on the quality, availability and safety of goods and services but unfortunately the consumers are still victims of unscrupulous and exploitative trade practices. Many of us are not aware about how and where to file a complaint if the manufacturer gives a defective product or deficiency in service or an adulterated food item.

The process of development along with the expanding globalisation and liberalisation process has increased the number of consumer related issues. Consumer protection has earned an important place in the political, economic and social agendas of many nations. In India, the Government has taken many steps including legislative, to protect consumers.Here lies the importance of educational institution in imparting the rights of the consumers. An aware consumer is an asset to the society. Seeking full information regarding quality and price of the goods and services and not buying blindly and demanding full information before buying is what an aware consumer do.

Education is the most powerful tool for the progress of the country and is a social and political necessity. Education helps an individual—as a consumer—in making rational choices and protects him from trade and business-related exploitation. But more is needed for the effective functioning of the national market to create an increased level of awareness of consumer rights, and for this consumers have to be educated about rights and responsibilities through concerted publicity and awareness campaigns. In the awareness campaigns, special emphasis needs to be given to vulnerable groups such as women and children, students, farmers and rural families and the working class. The report of the study on the Consumer Protection Act commissioned by the Comptroller and Auditor General (C & AG) of India, conducted in July-August 2005, brought out that 66 per cent of consumers were not aware of consumer rights and 82 per cent were not even aware of the Consumer Protection Act. In rural areas, only 13 per cent of the population had heard of the Consumer Protection Act.

Although implementation of the Consumer Protection Act can be viewed as a success, there are still serious shortfalls in achieving consumer awareness and protection. For imparting consumer education, schools and colleges in their elegant manner, may render the best help to consumer movement, a socio-economic movement, which is yet to take concrete and viable status in the state of Manipur in particular and the country in general. Designing the course-content at school level and at degree and diploma courses should be done to make the consumers aware of their right and protect themselves against any unfair trade practices. Training, seminar, talk show and various steps can be undertaken. Consumer education can take place in many ways. The Government and educational institutions have identified the importance of consumer education and gives support in many ways. Among all, educational institutions plays a vital role in the success of consumerism and consumer protection and awareness.

Literature Review

Akram (1994) stated that consumerism in our country has not yet reached the take off stage and a large number of Indian consumers are poor, illiterate, ignorant, ill-informed and unorganized. He highlights that in order to check this unhappy state of affairs, it is very important to educate the consumers about their rights.

ShobhaIyer (2002) in an article in *the Hindu*, consumer awareness at school level stated that schools must incorporate consumer education in school curricula as it is important to impart the practical skills and critical ability needed to cope with social and economic changes.

A.K.Vyas (2006) in his article consumer protection and welfare—Role of educational institutions in Manipur for *The Sangai Express* states that for imparting consumer education schools and colleges may be the best institutions and that course content should be designed to cover essential aspects of consumerism - social, economic, legal, moral and alien.

Objectives

1. To know the importance of Consumer Protection in the present scenario.
2. To explore the need for introducing consumer education in the basic curricula in an education system.
3. To find out the role of educational institution in protecting the consumers.

Methodology

The study is based on secondary data such as books, articles, and website.

Role of Educational Institutions in Consumer Protection in Manipur

Consumer awareness and education surely avoids exploitation as it is included by majority of the universities in their syllabus. Educational institutes are obtaining so many grants from UGC, AICTE and other government boards for conducting, seminars, conferences, books, and journals to bring the focus on consumer protection and awareness. To educate the present generation about Consumer Protection Act, consumer forums, agencies, courts and educational institutes have to play a vital role. Some of the role played by Indian educational institutions in promoting consumer protection and awareness are:

- The Central Board of Secondary Education has highlighted the guiding points of consumer protection and IGNO University has introduced a special course for both under graduate and post graduate students.
- Few schemes are under finalization for setting up National level projects in collaboration with leading consumer organizations, industry associations and academic institutions, like IITs, IIMs, IIPA, IIFT and reputed Central universities, are to provide consumer education, training and research on a more structured and sustained basis.
- A centre of Excellences is established by reputed organizations, like IITs and IIMs to facilitate action suits for major consumer problems. Many schools, colleges and universities are actively taking part in various schemes introduced by the government. Ex: *Grahak Jagaran.*
- A scheme was launched in 2002 to set up consumer club in each Middle/High/Higher Secondary School/College affiliated to a government recognized Board/University.

- Bureau of Indian Standards organizes education utilization of standard programmes in various educational institutes.
- Some reputed institutes like VIT University and IITs have courses like Indian Business Environment, Consumerism, and Consumer Protection. These institutes also conduct various campaigns in and around the university surroundings and are also doing many projects regarding consumer awareness through which they are in a position to analyse the sort of approach that people are expecting from the campaigns.
- Seminars, conferences, workshops, consumer festivals, research/evaluation studies are encouraged by various grants and the results are being published in the form of books, monographs and pamphlets on consumer education and awareness. The Indian Institute of Public Administration (IIPA), New Delhi, has been identified as the nodal organization to administer this scheme.
- A National Consumer Helpline project has been established in coordination with Delhi University, Department of Commerce in 2005. Consumers from all over the country can dial toll free number 1800-11-4000 and seek telephonic counselling for consumer problems.
- The students could make an impact by joining hands and questioning malpractices. As an aware consumer, students ought to rise above the backdrop of unscrupulous manufacturers and advertisers misleading the consumers. The main role of educational institutions is to create an aware future generation and this can be achieved by starting:
  - (a) Establishing Consumer Clubs which is a forum where students can be apprised about their consumer rights.
  - (b) Organizing talk show, training programmes, seminar and campaign in and outside their institutions.
  - (c) Maintaining an institutional magazine where consumer protection and awareness column be dedicated.

(d) Organizing competition among the students with the theme of consumer protection such as painting, extempore speech and debate etc. to make the students aware of the issues.

(e) Printing pamphlets or brochures explaining about consumer rights to the people and encourage them to boycott defective and bad quality goods which will spread market and product knowledge to the consumers.

Once the youth are aware of their rights and responsibities, the society along with various organizations can bring a solution to the issues of consumer protection.

Conclusion

The welfare of consumers remains in the hands of the consumers itself. If the consumers, particularly the young consumers whose number has been going up, are responsible, vigilant and are able to assert their rights and responsibilities, resist and reject substandard goods and services wherever required and also do not hesitate to seek justice through consumer courts if needed, the manufacturers, traders and service providers cannot afford to take them for granted while selling a product or rendering service on payment or to adopt any unfair trade practice. An alert consumer aware of his rights and responsibilities not only can protect himself but can also make consumer sovereignty a reality. The imparting of awareness and protection can start right from an early stage at schools, colleges and universities.

References

Akram, S. (1994). Consumer Protection in India under the shadow of Legislation, *The Indian Journal of Commerce*, Vol. XXXXVIII. No. 181, December.

PulidindiVenugopal, P. Vijayakumar & M.Varun Kumar (2012) Consumer Awareness and Role of Educational Institutions, *A Journal of Radix International Educational and Research Consortium*, Vol. 1, Issue 5 www.rierc.org

ShobhaIyer (2002). Consumer Awareness at School Level, *The Hindu*, Online edition of India's National Newspaper.

Consumer Awareness and Consumer Protection Act—A Study Sewanand *International Journal of Transformations in Business Management* http://www.ijtbm.com (IJTBM) 2012, Vol. No. 1, Issue No. 6, Apr-Jun.

Sadyojathappa S. (2017). Need of Consumer Protection Act in India in the Present Scenario, International Journal of Engineering Research and Development, Volume 13, Issue 9, pp. 55-58.www.ijerd.com

P. Uma Maheswari Devi, B. Sankara Rao. (2016). Consumer Protection Awareness—Role of Education, *Universal Journal of Industrial and Business Management* *4*(4): 97-103, http://www.hrpub.org DOI: 10.13189/ujibm.2016.040401

10

Consumer Protection in Manipur as Per UN Guidelines

Moirangthem Shanti Devi, Kangjam Mukhara Devi and *Thingbaijam Guneshwor*

Introduction

Consumer protection is particularly for the promotion, protection and education of the fundamental rights of the consumers. As we all know, the basic purpose of economic planning is to allocate resources for maximum satisfaction of consumer needs. Ultimately the goods and services produced in any economy are meant for the king of the market, i.e. the consumer. In the past history of India reveals, the needs and requirement of the people were absolutely few, simple and limited and as a result, there was no place of complexity either in production or in consumption. Same was the case regarding consumption activities also. Protection of the consumers was a less important aspect in those days.

But, gradually the market conditions and environment are changing with the growth of industrialisation, globalisation and liberalisation in the country. At present, the requirements of the consumers have grown enormously in quantity, quality and complexity. The various new products produced with the help of modern technological devices thrown in our markets, are of such nature in respect of which our consumers are completely ignorant and are unable to take their buying decisions without the help or assistance of some other sources, which cannot be taken to be granted as a genuine one always. As a result, making mankind aware about the quality of the consumer is a phenomenon which developed during the spectacular increase in the offer of goods and services and at the same time with the competition which has reached a very large level. In a developing country like India where the prevalence of poverty and unemployment is very high and level of literacy is very low, because of which people have to go through bulk of problems, notably in consumer related issues. Manipur, one of the eight states of North-eastern India, is not exceptional. Now-a-days, Manipur is a part of global market. Market functions mainly on twin factor—producers and consumers (Vyas, 2006). Various nefarious activities are involved right from starting point to using point. In the modern age of science and technology numerous are the ways of profiteering and cheating. In Manipur local goods are dependable but Manipur as a user State has to depend on Indian goods coming through national highways and outside goods coming through Moreh route (as Moreh is international market of Manipur) located in the border of Myanmar. So the issue of consumer protection is notable.

Objective

The objective of this chapter is to highlight the state of affairs of consumer protection in Manipur (one of the North-eastern states of India) by comparing the current status of the state with reference to the guidelines for consumer protection by United Nations (UN) or Consumers International. It states the major deviations between the consumer protection framework and its application, their drawbacks and the reasons behind it. It also highlights the need of Consumer Education. Lastly, it concludes with some recommendations that might improve the consumer protection in Manipur.

Consumer Protection Law

Consumer protection refers to the laws and other forms of government regulation designed to protect consumers. It is a group of laws and organisations meant to ensure the rights of consumers, as well as fair trade, competition, and accurate information in the marketplace. The laws are designed to prevent the businesses that engage in fraud or specified unfair practices in the market. In a rational economy, there is this logical, political, and moral force in the proposal that the consumers themselves should have the right to take and make decisions for fulfilling their needs with wise use of resources being allocated. However, the consumer protection appears as an important problem for the entire society. As a consequence the notion of consumers' rights starts taking shape in the 18th century but only later in the second half of the 19th century social actions and legislative efforts appeared. Realising this, the international organisation of consumer unions, now known as Consumers International took the action and under its consistent persuasion, the UN adopted a set of guidelines for the Consumer Protection on April 9, 1985 which were amended in 1999. The development of consumer protection law in India is mainly concerned with or related to some basic issues, like as enforcement of correct weight and measurement for the protection against the deceit in weights and measures ; fair trading standards, restrictions and restrictive trade practices for the prevention against malpractices in the area of business and trade; health and safety of the consumers for the protection against malnutrition and deterioration and degradation of the quality of the products etc.

The Indian consumers became conscious about the qualities and standards of different products, after the technological revolution that took place in the eighties. From this period, the consumer movement began to receive a momentum that was not there in the country earlier. During this period, various 'Consumer Associations' exerted their pressure upon the Government of India, in order to enact a specific legislation for the protection of the rights and interests of the consumers at large in the country. Thus the

Consumer Protection Act, 1986 (COPRA-1986) came into being with reference to the guidelines of UN. The aim and object as given in the 'Preamble' to the Act are to provide better protection of the interests and rights of the consumers and also to provide for the settlement of consumer disputes. The Act also provides safeguards against unfair trade practices by the manufacturers and sellers in the country. The Act was further amended by the Consumer Protection (Amendment) Act of 1993 seeking enlargement of the scope of areas covered under the Act and to entrust more powers to the redressal agencies. Although the Act has provided valuable opportunity to consumers to seek redressal of their grievances, the disposal of cases has not been fast enough. Several bottlenecks and shortcomings have come to light in the implementation of various provisions of the Act. With a view to achieve quicker and effective disposal of consumer complaints and to widen the scope of the Act, it was again amended by the Consumer Protection (Amendment) Act, 2002. As a consequence of the importance of the theme and of its presence in the life of mankind numerous causes were developed which support the necessity of a protection system for the rights and interests of the consumers. Thus it is important to understand definition of consumer under the Act.

Consumer

The term "consumer" has been defined in section 2(l)(d) of the Act. It is in two parts: the first part defines the "consumer" with reference to 'goods' and the second with reference to 'services'. According to this definition any purchaser of goods and hirer of services for a consideration comes under the purview of the definition of the consumer. It is not necessary that the consideration should have already been paid for the goods or services in question. For qualifying as a consumer, mere promise to pay the consideration is sufficient. So the purchaser of goods with deferred payment can also be treated as consumer. The users of goods and the beneficiaries of services other than the actual purchasers or hirers, who use or avail them with the approval of such purchasers or hirers, have been expressly declared as consumers under the definition of the consumer. Any person who purchases goods for resale or any "commercial purpose" has been excluded from the meaning of the term 'consumer'. The expression "commercial purpose" has not been defined in the Act. It has been left to be determined by judicial interpretation. Thus, to sum up the above brief explanation, a consumer is a person who buys or hires goods or services for consideration. Consumer is someone who acquires goods or services for direct use or ownership rather than for resale or use in production or manufacturing.

The UN adopted a set of guidelines for consumer protection which is very wide. It includes various rights and various remedies which are available to consumers. There are certain aspects of consumer protection:

- Promotion and protection of consumer's economic interest.
- Standards for safety and quality of consumer goods and services.
- Distribution facilities for essential consumer goods and services.
- Measures enabling consumers to obtain redress.
- Education and information programmes.
- Promotion of sustainable consumption.
- Measures relating to specific areas like water, food and pharmaceuticals.

As per the above mentioned guidelines, these are adapted into 8 consumer rights by Consumers International:

(a) Right to Basic Needs
(b) Right to Choice
(c) Right to Information
(d) Right to Safety
(e) Right to Consumer Education
(f) Right to Redressal
(g) Right to Representation
(h) Right to Healthy Environment

Right to Basic Needs

The UN guideline indirectly mentions the right to make basic needs for government to take adequate measures so that consumers can easily access the "basic needs for goods and services". The basic needs include food, clothing, health care, drinking water, sanitation, shelter, education, energy and transportation. There are 2 goods and 6 services included in the basic needs. To cite an instance, in India, the Central Government for ensuring food security (Right to Food) introduced Public Distribution System (PDS). The minor failures of PDS in Manipur relate to factors such as low margins of Fair Price Shop owners, which lead to corruption, transportation bottlenecks and timings of the opening of shops not being convenient.

Right to Choice

According to this right every consumer has the right to choose the goods or services. This means an assurance of availability, ability and access to variety of products and services at competitive price and by competitive price we mean just and fair price. UN guidelines deal with economic aspects under its section on promotion and protection of consumer's economic interest. In India, the considerable legislations are approving MRTP Act, 1969, Bureau of Indian Standards Act, 1986 and Weight Measure Act. A new competition law 'Competition Act, 2002' which has replaced MRTP Act, is being introduced. However, factors like limited information about products, preconceived notions, and absence of effective regulatory mechanism prevent the consumers in Manipur to follow and take actions.

Right to Information

The consumer has the right to get information about the quality, quantity, purity, standard and price of goods and services so as to protect himself/herself against the abusive trade practices and making right decisions. Consumers should also have the right to access information regarding public affairs as well as those which are handled by government and its agencies and hence Right to

Information Act, 2005 has been introduced. The department of consumer affairs has taken certain steps to provide information to the public. An intensive multimedia consumer campaign "*Jaago Grahak Jaago*!" is being telecast regularly to make the consumers aware of their rights and duties. National Consumer Helpline has started for easy filing of complaints. However, the inter-play of many institutions/ministries with little co-ordination is the major hurdle in the way of implementation of these laws in Manipur.

Right to Safety

The consumers have the right to be protected against the marketing of goods and services which are hazardous to life and property. Two aspects of safety under UN guidelines are:

(a) Physical Safety and Standards of safety.
(b) Quality of consumer goods and service.

Under the constitutional provisions, the most essential one is the Protection of Life & Personal Liberty (Article 21). Under the legislative provisions, the crucial ones are Prevention of Food Adulteration Act, 1954 and Bureau of Indian Standard Act, 1986. Even though the categorizing certain products to comply to Indian Standard Institution (ISI) and FSSAI norms and regulations, still many products in the market are without these marks. In Manipur, there are unlimited products without the marks which mean not adhering to the prevailing norms. They are even unaware of whom to approach in case they face any problem regarding safety. Prevailing corruption in the administrative system makes the laws ineffective in many such cases.

Right to Consumer Education

It is the right of consumer to acquire the knowledge and skills to be informed to customers. Along with the aim to educate the consumers to know their rights and take actions, this right also assures that illiterate consumer can seek information about the existing acts and agencies that are being set up for their protection.

However, as of now there is not any definit policy in India concerning consumer education, so is the same scenario in the state. Under the directive of the Government of India, consumer education has been included in the school curriculum. The NCERT is working on introducing consumer education in the syllabus. The IGNOU has devised a syllabus for distant education on consumer protection as a separate course. Despite provision taken by Government of India and consumer organisations, still mass public of Manipur are unaware or partially aware about legislations and implementation of consumer protection mechanism. Our traditional education system does not teach students about consumer awareness, consumer rights, consumer laws etc. At the same time, consumer protection education is included in syllabus in some limited courses in colleges and University in Manipur. Hence, many students do not know about grievance redressal system, consumer protection act, consumerism, consumer fund, consumer co-operatives etc.

Right to Redressal

According to right, it includes right to be compensated for misrepresentation of unsafe/deficient goods or unsatisfactory services and availing the acceptable forms of legal aid or redressal for small claims. Three tier Quasi-Judicial Machinery is set up at each district, state and national levels called District Forums, State Consumer Redressal Commission and National Commission (or National Consumer Disputes Redressal Commission) respectively. Despite the establishment of such comprehensive law, the scenario of consumer redressal in Manipur is constrained with complications like non-compliance with order, delays in judgement etc. But it is worth mentioning that the current scenario shows a tremendous improvement from the previous situations.

Right to Representation

In this, the consumer has the right to represent himself or to be heard or to advocate his interest. In case a consumer has been exploited or has any complaint against the product or service then he has the right to be heard and be assured that his/her interest would receive due consideration. According to the UN guidelines, the government should encourage the development of independent consumer groups for presenting the views in the decision making process. In India, government has set up Parliament Commission and representation mechanism in various departments. The Directorate of Public Grievances handles complaint that is addressed to the Central Government. Further, any individual or group can seek remedies through representation by filing written petitions in the Supreme Court or High Court. However, the major issue associated with representation is the corruption in the system, which leads to delays in getting justice. There is also lack of effective co-ordination between consumer organisations for smooth implementation.

Right to Healthy Environment

As per this right, the consumer and all the citizens have the right to be protected against the environmental pollution and environmental degradation. Under the UN guidelines, government must adopt measures to use, store and production of pesticides and chemicals. This is now listed as a consumer right. Introduction of Environment Act, 1986 provides the instructions for management of hazardous wastes etc. for example—safety reports, safety audit etc. It also includes pollution of water, air and soil. The Pollution Control Board of Manipur is the apex body that monitors the pollution level in Manipur as well as it has its norms and regulations. The main issue is the lack of awareness among consumers in Manipur regarding hazardous use of pesticides, chemicals and vehicle traffic. Besides, ineffective training of people add to the problem.

Concluding Remark

From the above discussion, it can be concluded that in Manipur, it is not the legislative part that is inadequate in administering the consumer protection mechanism of rights and laws. The actual challenge lies in strengthening the administrative mechanism in achieving such measures. Another challenge is the lack of resources especially the manpower to perform their duties and providing incentives for these officials without feeling handicapped due to lack of resources is a major challenge. Most importantly government should impose punishment and fines to food adulterers, hoarders, black marketers of necessary consumer goods and services. As such severe penalties should be imposed, that it acts as a big discouragement for such criminals or defaulters. Of all challenges, the major issue to be concerned is about consumer education. The success any legislation, laws, programmes, schemes and basically rights depends on consumer education. Until and unless consumers are motivated and empowered to take initiative in the development process, the rights, laws and programmes which are implemented by the government cannot succeed. Besides we can see the outcomes are not that favourable. For a strong Consumer Movement, legislations and laws alone will not suffice. Consumer education is the key to make the movement a success. Course content, starting right from the school to higher education, should be designed to cover essential aspects of consumerism socially, economically, legally, and ethically. Ultimately, it is the consumer whose proactive actions can help spread the message that no one can short change them.

References

Government of India, *The Consumer Protection Act, 1986.*

United Nations, *Guidelines for Consumer Protection*, April 9, 1985.

United Nations, General Assembly *Resolution No.: 39/248*, revised in 1999.

United Nations, 2003, *Guidelines for Consumer Protection*, as expanded in 1999, Department of Social and Economic Welfare, New York.

Vyas, A.K. (2006). Consumer Protection and Welfare, Role of Educational Institutions in Manipur, *The Sangai Express*, August 4, 2006.

11

Need of Consumer Awareness

An Educated Person is Not Necessarily an Aware Consumer

G.P. Prasain and *W. Priyokumar Singh*

Introduction

Customer is the fulcrum of all business activities and also the only person subjected to all types of exploitation. With the advancement of technology and changing expectations of consumers the business men are adopting various strategies to earn their profits at the cost of the customer in order to meet the increasing competition. In spite of the best consumer laws and serious measures of the government to protect the interests of the consumers, exploitation is increasing day by day. The major reason contributing to this situation is lack of awareness among the Consumers about their rights and protection measures. The Consumer Protection Act is a compassionate social legislation that provides for protection of rights of the consumers and redressal of consumer disputes. CPA has provided for three tier quasi-judicial consumer dispute redressal mechanism at district, state and national level. The Act applies to all goods and services, excluding goods for resale or for commercial purpose, services rendered free of charge and under a contract for personal service. In spite of these Consumer Protection Acts and measures, consumers are still being exploited and the main reason is lack of awareness.

In this scenario an attempt is made in this chapter to study the awareness level of consumers about consumer protection, their buying, practices and perceptions of consumers about their rights.

Objectives of Study

The following are the main objectives of the study:

- To study the awareness of the educated consumers about consumer protection.
- To study the responsibility of educated consumer for his safeguard.
- To study what laws existed before the enactment of Consumer Protection Act, 1986?

Methodology of the Study

Keeping in view the objectives of the study, it is proposed to carry out the investigation and to collect the Primary data. A structured questionnaire was administered to the twenty consumers in the Imphal East and Imphal West. The questions were designed in 'Yes' or 'No' about the awareness of consumer rights, demanding of the bill or cash memo from the sellers, checking cash memo or bill, asking the seller to specify local tax, checking the date of manufacture and date of expiry, awareness of BIS (Bureau of Indian Standards) and AGMARK, awareness of legislations to protect consumers, criteria in choosing goods and availability of consumer organization.

Analytical Tools

Statistical techniques like percentage and average have been adopted for the purpose of analyzing data. Calculations are made through computer by using "Excel".

According to Sec. (1) (d) of Consumer Protection Act, 1986, consumer means any person who (i) buys any goods for a consideration, which has been paid or promised in partly paid and partly promised. It also includes —(a) user of such goods who is using the goods with permission of the buyer or (b) person who has obtained goods under any system of deferred payment. Person who has obtained goods for resale or for commercial purposes is not covered under this section.

In brief consumer means any person who might wish to be supplied with the goods for his own private use or consumption. Before the enactment of Consumer Protection Act, 1986, there were some major laws in India. They are:

1. *Indian Penal Code, 1860*—Some sections of Indian Penal Code, viz. 264-267 and 269-278 relates to fraudulent use of weights and measures, spreading of infection, adulteration of food or drugs, and voluntary corrupting or flouting of water public spring or reservoir.
2. *Indian Contract Act, 1872*—Provides to see that a man or woman fulfills what he or she promises to his or her fellow being.
3. *Sale of Goods Act, 1930*—Contact of sale, conditions and warranties in the sale, transfer of property between seller and buyer, duties of seller and buyer, rights of unpaid sellers against the goods suits for the breach of the contract.
4. *Drugs and Cosmetics Act, 1940 (Amendment 1982)*—Prohibits the import, manufacture, distribution and sale of substandard drugs.
5. *Drugs (Control) Act, 1950*—Related to the control of the supply, sale and distribution of drugs.
6. *Industries (Development and Regulation) Act, 1951*—Provides for the development and regulations of certain industries.
7. *Indian Standard Institution (Certification Marks) Act, 1952*—Provides for the standardization and marking of goods which is a prerequisite to the establishment of a healthy trade and to compare favorably with the established marks of foreign products.

8. *Drugs and Magic (Objectionable Advertisements) Act, 1954*—Prohibition of advertisement of certain drugs for treatment of certain diseases and disorders.
9. *Prevention of Food Adulteration Act, 1954 (Amendment 1964)*—Provides to curb the increasing tendencies in adulteration of food stuffs.
10. *Essential Commodities Act, 1955 (Amendment 1966, 1967, 1971, 1974, 1976, 1981 and 1984)*—Provides for the control of production, supply anddistribution of certain commodities in the trade and commerce.
11. *Trade and Merchandise Marks Act, 1958*—Provides for the registration, better protection of trademarks and for the prevention of the use of fraudulent marks on merchandise.
12. *Specific Relief Act, 1963*—Some sections of the Act provides for reliefs obtainable in civil courts.
13. *Monopolies and Restrictive Practices Act, 1969 (Amendment 1984 and 1991)*—Trade Provides that the operation of economic system does not result in the concentration of economic power to the common determinant.
14. *Hire-Purchase Act, 1972*—Provides special protection to a hirer wherever such protection is legitimately and inevitably needed.
15. *Code of Criminal Procedure Act, 1973*—Section 153 of the Code Pronounces that the police is empowered to check the weights and measures without any warrant.
16. *Cigarettes (Regulation of Production, Supply and Distribution) Act, 1975*—Provides to regulate trade and commerce, production, supply and distribution of cigarettes.
17. *Standards of Weights and Measure Act, 1976*—Provide for establishment of standards of weight and measures on metric system, regulation of interstate trade or commerce in weights, measures and other goods which are sold or distributed.

18. *Prevention of Black-Marketing and Maintenance of Supplies of Essential Commodities Act, 1980*—It prevent malpractices such as black-marketing, hoarding, profiteering and unjustified price rises of essential commodities.
19. *Narcotic Drugs and Psychotropic Substances Act, 1985*—Relates to control and regulation of narcotic and psychotropic substances and other related matter.

From the above laws one can observe that there are numerous laws in order to protect the interests of the consumer. However, due to lack of proper implementation of laws and also as majority of laws are non-compensatory in nature one needs to stress the need for enactment of the Consumer Protection Act, 1986, which is compensatory in nature, in order to protect the interests of the consumers.

There are some more independent Regulatory Agencies by 'Executive Branch Department' which protect the public interest and create awareness among the people:

1. Federal Trade Commission (FTC)
2. Consumer Products Safety Commission (CPSC)
3. Environmental Protection Agency (EPA)
4. Federal Communications Commission (FCC)
5. Interstate Commerce Commission (FCC)
6. Federal Maritime Commission (FMC)
7. Securities and Exchange Commission (SEC)
8. Commodity Futures Trade Commission (CFTC)
9. International Trade Commission (ITC)
10. Consumer Financial Protection Bureau (CRPB)
11. Food and Drug Administration (FDA)
12. National Highway Traffic Safety Administration (NHTSA).

Reasons for Unawareness

The above agencies or commissions are not known to educate consumers. The following are the main reasons for ignorance of the educated consumers.

(a) **Lack of Consumer Education:** There is no board or university, which teaches a student about consumer's rights and market conditions. So, students remain unaware despite being educated. They do not get proper knowledge about the products, which they want to purchase. There are so many parts of education, which can protect a consumer.

(i) **Proper lecturers:** There is lack of proper guidance to consumers. There are no lecture in any university about consumer's protection.

(ii) **Seminars:** There are many seminars on this topic. Seminars can play a big role to educate a consumer but there are no proper arrangements of seminars on consumer's protection.

(iii) **Academic Curriculum:** Consumer protection is not a subject in our academic curriculum. So, students despite being educated are unaware about their rights as consumer.

(b) **Unawareness about consumer's rights:** Large number of consumers may have heard about the Consumer Act and redressal agencies but they do not make use of them, as they do not know how to lodge a complaint, where to go and how to go about.

(c) **Cunning producers:** Today's producers are so cunning that they think only about their own profits. For this reason, they give wrong descriptions about their products through media and create misinformation among educated and uneducated.

(d) **Variety of products:** There are so many companies of one product that an educated consumer is also confused about the product. He remains puzzled. So he is not aware about every aspect of the product for price, quality, quantity, brand etc. which he is going to purchase. For example, in the market, variety of shampoos is available. It is not easy task to know the details of every shampoo product.

(e) **Lack of time:** In the fast paced life, man is so busy that he has not time to be aware. He does not go from shop to shop to purchase goods/services. So he remains unaware about the actual price and quality of the product and is exploited from the hands of sellers.

(f) **Improper response of the salesman:** If an educated consumer wants to be aware about a product, the salesman does not give him proper information. This creates unawareness among the consumers about their products. Actually, sellers want that buyer always remains unaware.

(g) **Lack of awareness by the Government:** Very few efforts have been made by the government to create awareness. If an educated person wants to be aware about market and products, there is no other source for him except a salesman (who does not give right information to him).

(h) **Poverty:** Poverty is another cause of ignorance. A poor person, though he is educated yet take no interest in their problems as consumer. If his family needs basic things of life then he will think about to protect his family first.

Survey of Awareness of an Educated Consumer

A survey was performed on the twenty educated persons to check their awareness about consumer's right and consumerism. I interviewed and asked about the awareness of consumer rights, demanding cash memo or bill for purchase of goods, checking the totals of cash memo or bill, comparing the actual rate paid with the Maximum Retail Price rate, asking the seller to specify local tax, checking the date of manufacture and expiry, awareness of Bureau of Indian Standard (BIS) and AGMARK, awareness of legislations to protect consumers, criteria in choosing goods and availability of consumer organization.

The answers were analysed, clubbed and tabulated as shown below.

Table 11.1: Scores of Educated Consumer Awareness and their Percentage

Sl. No.	Components	Scores		Total	% of Yes	% of No
		Yes %	No %			
1	Awareness of consumer rights	15	5	20	75	25
2	Cash memo or bill from sellers	3	17	20	15	85
3	Checking cash memo or bill	6	14	20	30	70
4	Comparing the actual rate paid with the MRP rate	9	11	20	45	55
5	Asking the seller to specify local tax	4	16	20	20	80
6	Checking the date of manufacture and date of expiry	16	4	20	80	20
7	Awareness of BIS and AGMARK	15	5	20	75	25
8	Awareness of legislations to protect consumers	13	7	20	65	35
9	Criteria in choosing goods	6	14	20	30	70
10	Availability of consumer organization	3	17	20	15	85
	Total	**90**	**110**	**Total**	**450**	**550**
	Percentage to the total	**45**	**55**	**Average**	**225**	**275**

From the above table it was found that aware consumers were 45 per cent and unaware consumer were 55 per cent. It means that educated consumers are less aware. Out of the 20 educated consumers, there are 75 per cent consumers who are aware about consumer rights and 25 per cent consumers are unaware about consumer rights. There are only 15 per cent consumers from the 20 educated consumers who demand the bill or cash memo from the sellers and 85 per cent consumers are unaware about the bill or

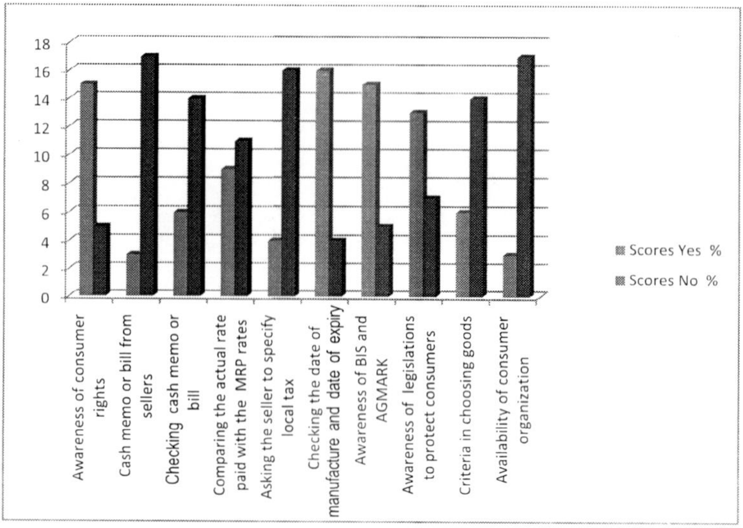

Fig. 11.1: Graph showing the scores of educated consumer

cash memo from the sellers. Among the 20 educated consumers, the scores of yes are checking cash memo or bill 30 per cent, comparing the actual rate paid with the MRP rate 45 per cent, asking the seller to specify local tax 20 per cent, checking the date of manufacture and date of expiry 80 per cent, awareness of BIS and AGMARK 75 per cent, awareness of legislations to protect consumers 65 per cent, criteria in choosing goods 30 per cent and availability of consumer organization 15 per cent. Among the 20 educated consumers, the scores of No are checking cash memo or bill 70 per cent, comparing the actual rate paid with the MRP rate 55 per cent, asking the seller to specify local tax 80 per cent, checking the date of manufacture and date of expiry 20 per cent, awareness of BIS and AGMARK 25 per cent, awareness of legislations to protect consumers 35 per cent, criteria in choosing goods 70 per cent and availability of consumer organization 85 per cent. The maximum score of yes is 75 per cent and No is 85 per cent which is represented by awareness of consumer rights and demanding bills from sellers. The minimum score of Yes is 15 per cent. It is represented by the two items, i.e. demand the bill or cash memo from the sellers and availability of consumer organization. On the other hand, the minimum score of No is checking the date of manufacture and date of expiry which is represented by 20 per cent.

By overall performance of the analysis, it can be concluded that only 45 per cent educated consumers are aware and the remaining, i.e. 55 per cent unaware about their rights as consumers. On the other hand the average of total percentage of unaware educated consumer is 275 whereas the aware educated consumer is 225 only.

Responsibilities of Educated Consumers to Protect

The following are the responsibilities of an educated consumer while purchasing from the market:

1. The consumer himself should make all buying decisions.
2. While making a purchase he should make efforts to obtain the information about the details of the product and services.
3. It is the responsibility of the consumer to keep the receipts and other relevant documents for future reference especially for durable goods.
4. He should not buy more than his requirements, which will lead to hoarding.
5. An educated consumer should study the price range and the quality that he is looking for or whether they are acceptable to him.
6. It is also an important responsibility of educated consumer to know about the production process and marketing of goods properly.
7. Educated consumer should investigate deeply about his problems as consumer. It is a big responsibility of self-help.
8. He should go shop to shop and place to place to know about the real price, quality and quantity of product.

Suggestions to Aware Educate the Consumer

As a consumer, he must be aware of his basic rights and should fight for those rights. The followings are the some suggestions to enlighten the educated consumer:

1. **Consumer Education:** An educated consumer should be educated to visit more shops before purchasing any product and they should be made to understand the significance of demanding receipts for the paymentsmade. Frequent exhibitions and demonstrations should be organized in many public places to highlight the consumer's rights, the unfair trade practices of the traders and so on.
2. **Part of Study:** The topic of consumer awareness should be the part of our education. For this reason, educational institutions should introduce consumer education as the subject in their academic curricula effective steps should be taken to encourage youth to take active part in the activities of consumer movements.
3. **Role of Media:** There should be a consumer education campaign through various communication media such as posters, publications, radio, television, films, lectures, seminars and workshop training etc. for an educated consumer.
4. **Role of Consumer Organizations:** Consumer organizations should impart training to the consumers to identify their rights and grievances. In this connection, the government should take effective steps with the support of consumer organizations to celebrate the Consumer Day on 15th March every year in all parts of the state especially in educational institutions. Consumer organizations should form their own federation at the district level.
5. **Centre for Consumer Protection at University Level:** A centre for consumer protection should be established at the university level, with the objective of creating consumer awareness among the students. It should familiarize the

students with legal rights of consumers and procedures for redressal of consumer grievances.

6. **Market condition:** Appropriate centres should be established at all market yards or district headquarters to enable the educated consumer to test the goods purchased by them and check the weight and measure.
7. **Efforts by government to enlighten an educated consumer:** A citizens' charter and public utilities commission for the country should be established effectively by the government, so as to improve the quality, choice, standards and value of public services.
8. **Awareness about consumer legislations:** Government should teach/guide an educated consumer about consumer legislation (consumer courts, consumer agencies etc.). Example, if an educated consumer wants to be aware of some products and salesmen do not give him proper information. So, he may claim the same through consumer legislation.
9. **Self Help:** Consumer should help himself. He should demand bills and check those bills after purchase. He should know all about the price of that commodity which he is going to purchase.
10. **Educated consumer:** Consumer should be educated to join voluntarily the consumer co-operative as members and use the society to safeguard their interest by availing the services at reasonable cost.

Conclusion

From this study, it can be concluded that an educated consumer can also be an unaware consumer. But there are many reasons for his unawareness as give in this chapter. For this reason, there are some suggestions in the chapter. An educated consumer should follow these suggestions and responsibilities so that he is cautions while purchasing goods/services from the market.

12

Consumer Protection and Financial Literacy for Adult Learners

Sharmila Thingbaijam

Literacy and Consumer Protection

The need of adult education is being increasingly recognized, particularly in the areas of development. Without literacy we cannot improve the level of living, the socio-economic status, the political system, life style, the process of development, human resource development and ultimately, the quality of lives of the people. Literacy will improve knowledge, attitudes and skills, politicize, provide pride in self, and in cultural identity, and prepare people for self-generated change. Consumer protection ensures that consumers receive information that will allow them to make informed decisions and are not subjected to unfair and deceptive practices have access to recourse mechanisms to resolve disputes when transactions go awry and are able to maintain privacy of their personal information. Now-a-day it is widely acknowledged that the level of consumer awareness and protection is true indicator of development of the country and progressiveness of civil society. The main reason for this is the rapidly increasing variety of goods and services which modern technology has made available, the high level of sophistication in marketing and selling practices and in advertising and other forms of promotion, mass marketing methods and consumers increased mobility. This has resulted in reduction of personal interaction between buyers and sellers, and contributed to the increased need for consumer protection. In recent year's rural market have acquired significance in the overall growth of the economy and led to substantial increase in the purchasing power of the rural community.

The concern in the Constitution of India for protection and promotion of an individual's right, and for the dignity and welfare of the citizen makes it imperative to provide for the welfare of the individual as a consumer, a client and a customer. The consumer protection policy creates an environment whereby the clients, customers, and consumers receive satisfaction from the delivery of goods and services needed by them. Good governance requires efficiency, effectiveness, ethics, equality, economy, transparency, accountability, empowerment, rationality, impartiality and participation of citizens. The concern of consumer protection is to ensure fair trade practices, quality of goods and efficient services with information to the consumer with regard to quality, quantity, potency, composition and price for their choice of purchase. Thus, proper and effective implementation of consumer protection law promotes good governance but all of this will be impossible without literacy.

As the largest consumer base is in the rural areas, protecting the rural consumer has to be a priority in any strategy to protect the consumers. The concept of homogeneity of rural consumer specially the illiterate adult has posed a serious problem in formulating appropriate strategies to protect the rural consumers. There is also a perception that the rural people are only price conscious, not quality conscious. The biggest market for fakes is the rural markets. So, proper awareness is necessary among the rural people specially the adult illiterate about the consumer right for their social and economic development in the society.

Exploitation of the Illiterate People by the Business Community in the Rural Areas

The rural people are mostly illiterate and with the growth of rural markets and due to poor knowledge about their rights and also the lack of skills to take a rational decision based on information about the product or services, the rural people are exploited in many ways. The illiterate people haves been made to endure sub-standard products and services, adulterated foods, short weights and measures, spurious and hazardous drugs, exorbitant prices, endemic shortage leading to black marketing and profiteering, unfulfilled manufacturing guarantees and host of other ills. The rural people who generally depend on weekly markets to purchase essential things are often cheated due to lack of choice.

The rural people or consumers are generally ignorant and they are also unorganized. Thus, they are exploited by the manufacturers, traders, retailers and the service providers in different ways. The manufacturers and the traders take advantage of the condition of the rural consumers. The rural people face various problems like adulteration, short weighing and measuring, lack of safety and quality control in appliances and equipment, electrical and mechanical, unfair warranties and guarantees, imitation and unreasonable pricing etc. But for all this, the root cause is illiteracy that is why; in every field literacy is quite necessary so as to develop themselves and also to raise their living standard.

Need of Literacy and Empowerment among the Rural People for Consumer Protection

The consumers, while purchasing goods and services in the marketplace, are exploited in various ways. The main reason for such exploitation is illiteracy and ignorance. In the emerging scenario it is necessary to protect the rural people by educating them about their rights and empowering them to make decisions based on information about the goods and services. Awareness has to be created among the rural people or consumers. So far the consumer movement has largely been confined to the urban centers, and with the expanding rural markets now the focus has to shift to protect the rural consumer. Therefore, in the literacy classes of *Saakshar Bharat* programme, the adult learners should be taught the meaning of consumer awareness about—I: Maximum Retail Price (MRP). II: Fair Price Shop. III: Price, quality and expiry date of the products. IV: their rights and duties. V: Consumer Protection Act of 1986. VI: the certified products like ISI, Agmark, ISO-2000 etc. The common ways by which the consumers are exploited by the business community should be introduced in the curriculum of the adult education programmes.

Financial Literacy and Consumer Protection

Financial Literacy is "the ability to make informed judgments and to take effective actions regarding the current and future use and management of money. It includes the ability to understand financial choices, plan for the future, and spend wisely, and manage the challenges associated with life events such as a job loss, saving for retirement, or paying for child's education." It helps to make informed decisions and well-being of an individual. In today's world which has a market with complicated products, the need for financial literacy becomes inevitable and literacy goes beyond the provision of financial information and advice. It is the ability to know, monitor, and effectively use financial resources to enhance the well-being and economic security of an individual, their family, and business. The OECD defines financial literacy as—"A combination of awareness, knowledge, skill, attitude and behaviour necessary to make sound financial decisions and ultimately achieve individual financial well-being." Financial literacy helps consumers understand the information and make risk/return choices that optimize their financial wealth. In addition, consumer protection and financial literacy help promote deepening of the retail financial sector, attracting first-time consumers to access financial services and building public trust in financial institutions. Across the financial sector, consumer protection and financial literacy promote financial inclusion and use of financial services.

Despite noteworthy performance in a short span since its inception, "*Saakshar Bharat*" programme is still accosted with a few strategic limitations. Therefore, Government of India felt that it is imperative to launch a campaign to reinforce the philosophy, sprit and conceptual vision of *Saakshar Bharat* especially at Gram Panchayat level with new convergence partners to orient, enthuse, involve and activate stakeholders of *Saakshar Bharat* programme. Accordingly, interpersonal media campaign was launched in July 2013 as per discussions held during Quarterly Review Meeting of SLMAs, SRCs and NLMA held on 8-9 July, 2013 at Delhi. The interpersonal Media Campaign aims to cover electoral literacy, financial literacy, legal literacy, disaster management etc. under *Saakshar Bharat* programme.

Factors influencing financial literacy of marginalized adult learners are:

- **Knowledge:** Knowledge about financial products, proper formal education, basic money management skills, financial numeracy, persuasion knowledge and self-efficacy and basic banking activities.
- **Financial Behaviour:** Budgeting, trusted financial advice, cultural dominance and learned helplessness.
- **Financial Attitude:** Risk aversion, Retirement planning and their intensity to save.

An individual is said to be financially literate if he/she is able to perform the following:

- **Financial knowledge and understanding:** The individual should be aware of the products available in the market. He/she should possess adequate knowledge about the basics of the products, the related concepts, consumer rights of such products and its use.
- **Choosing appropriate products:** Should be able to compare similar products and choose the product which suits their requirement. Financial knowledge about the various products would enable this.

- **Financial Planning:** The intensity to save and plan for their retirement life should be clear. Investing in proper avenues or saving through various investment plans shows their attitude and behaviour towards financial matters. The studies listed above show that the financial attitude and behaviour is highly influenced by financial knowledge possessed by an individual.
- **Day-to-day Money Management:** Financial literacy helps an individual to have control over his financial matters. It enables an individual to frame appropriate budgets which in turn helps them to track his finances and meet the ends.

The need of financial literacy in our country has gained importance because of low level of literacy and large section of population which is excluded from financial set up. Complicated financial products, low level of awareness and lack of knowledge about financial matters makes the need for financial literacy significant. Literacy always helps to solve the problems and in inculcating confidence, claims and approach for their rights. Since India has a higher young demographic dividend, the study would help to know the need or steps to be taken to improve or update the existing financial literacy for consumer protection especially among the adult learners. Since the lack of literacy and lack of experience with financial products have resulted in poor management of finance, this kind of study would help them to improve in financial matters. Hence, the importance of literacy, financial literacy always arises among the adult learners in particular and other in general which empower all to exercise right to the consumer protection and to use their roles and responsibilities to enhance the status of economy in the society.

References

Abraham, Ansong, Michael Asiedu Gyensare (2012). Determinants of University Working-Students' Financial Literacy at the University of Cape Coast, Ghana, *International Journal of Business and Management*, 7(9), 126-135.

Falahati, L. and Paim, L. (2011). Gender Differences in Financial well-being among College Students. *Australian Journal of Basic and Applied Sciences, 5*(9), 1765-76.

Jago Grahak Jago. (2009). *Yojana.* A Development Monthly. Consumer Rights, February.

Lusardi, A., Mitchell, O.S., and Curto, V. (2010). Financial Literacy among the Young. *Journal of Consumer Affairs, 44*(2), 358-80.

Ronald, A. Sages, John, E. Grable (2010). Financial Numeracy, Net Worth, and Financial Management Skills: Client Characteristics That Differ Based on Financial Risk Tolerance. *Journal of Financial Service Professionals,* 57-65.

Tyagi, Vandana (2014). Consumer Protection Laws and Deceptive Marketing. *Review Journal of Political Philosophy,* Vol. 11, No.1, May.

13

Dynamic Equation of Bandhs and Blockades

Challenges to Consumers in Manipur, India

Partakson Romun Chiru and *Kh. Tomba Singh*

Introduction

The state has been losing over Rs. 1672.9 crore per day on every bandh or general strike and Rs. 943.33 crore per day in every economic blockade (Serto, 2017). There were 103 days of economic blockades in 2016 and 76 days till March 2017. Therefore, total loss in 2016 and 2017 due to strikes and bandhs and blockades is Rs. 2616.23 crore (Serto, 2017). Of the total 365 days, there were 224 days affected by the bandhs and blockades in 2010 in the state which means Rs. 211305.92 crore loss (224 days x 943.33 crore) during this year. Instability of economy transition in the state is what supresses the economy growth and resulted the economy victims squarely on the consumers.

Manipur is connected by road to the rest of India and to Myanmar by three national highways (NH-39, NH-53 and NH-153). Several hundred trucks ply on this route daily bringing essential commodities such as food grains, petrol, diesel, cooking gas etc.., from other parts of the country (Singh, A.M., 2007). As evident, such bandhs and blockades have had an adverse impact on Manipur economy. According to Indian Oil Corporation Limited, Petroleum product (POL, 2009), the economic impact of bandhs and blockades during 2010-11 was estimated at about Rs. 206.8 crore, while the total economic loss due to the blockades on highways was estimated at about Rs. 239.2 crore. The total loss was Rs. 446 crore, the same study estimated that during 2011-12 the total loss caused by bandhs and blockades was Rs. 553.23 crore. And estimated loss for 2012-13 was Rs. 520.73 crore.

Important Facts of Bandhs and Blockades in Manipur

(a) Nineteen (19) eposides of Bandhs and Blockades for over two hundred and twenty four (224) days along the National Highways (NH 39 & 53) in the year 2010.

(b) 273 different kinds of Bandhs and Blockades affecting 936 days during 1970 to March 2000, with available data in the State Archives, (in the year 2009) Government of Manipur.

(c) A debate was organised by "IPATHOUKOK" a voluntary organisation of Naoremthong on 1983.

(d) Rally against Bandh was also organised in Bishnupur District Headquarters in the year 1999.

(e) "The Supreme Court had banned Bandhs in 1998. In 2004, the Supreme Court fined the Bharatiya Janata Party and Shiva-Sena for organising a Bandh in Mumbai against bomb blast in the city."

(f) In Manipur, the Government also banned this kind of medium of expression on 28th August, 1999.

(g) A 7-Member House Committee was constituted to control Bandhs and Blockades in the State Assembly session in 2010 with (1) Th. Debendro Singh, (2) O. Joy Singh, (3) Radhabinod Koijam, (4) R.K. Ananda Singh, (5) Dr. Kh. Loken, (6) L Nandakumar, and 7. Dr. Kh. Ratankumar Singh.

Statement of the Problem

There were a lot of debates to find out the real reasons on issues like open games of underweight practices in the market; open adulteration in all items of food of daily consumption; the expired drugs and the consciousness of heavy premium paid by consumers on account of economic blockade. Therefore, the present study is initiated to focus on the existing position as well as future prospect of consumer behaviour in Manipur. Hence, entitled as "Dynamic Equation of Bandhs and Blockades and Challenges of Consumers Buying Behaviour in Manipur."

Review of Literature

Singh, A.M. (2007) states that Manipur have only three lifelines of National Highways, bandhs and Blockades of these Highways have been the most common practices to pressure the State Government. However, it resulted in scarcity of essential commodity and leads to economic loss of several crores of rupees.

Rahman, J. (2014) determined that the state has experience with many conflicts between various ethnic groups, He further maintained that there are economic implication of ethnic conflicts in the state. The valley life is frequently disturbed by the occurrence of bandhs, strike and economic blockades. This affects the economic condition of people of Manipur and thereby makes them poor.

Turner, K. and Krizek, R.L. (2006) presented that the organization, individual behavioural decision can be made by depending on those satisfaction or dissatisfaction, positive or negative experience or better treatment offer by the doctor can be effected not only the level of satisfactions also longer connectivity with customer. An individual ability to achieve satisfaction was mitigated by those service dimensions that created dissatisfaction as well as the order in which the individual service dimension. Taking a meaning—centre approach to customers' satisfaction or any other organization construct, place the lived experience and meaning that hold above the experiment at the centre that comes to understands what construct such a satisfaction means rather than what we have reified them by acknowledging the act of meaning creation.

Research Gap

From the above literature review, it shows that few studies were conducted so far in Manipur in particular to the hill region. Despite Manipur state being gifted with many resources and having tremendous commercial importance. Therefore, this topic is being chosen for present study, as it was felt that state was frequent victim of bandhs and blockades.

Objectives of the Study

1. To find the influence of socio-economic demographic (SED) of consumers on purchase behaviour during bandhs and blockades.
2. To analyse the impact of bandhs and blockades on buying behaviour of consumers.
3. To extend appropriate suggestion based on the findings of the study.

Hypothesis of the Study

Null Hypothesis H_0: There is no significant relationship between the bandhs and blockades and the buying behaviour of the consumers.

Methodology of the Study

Data collection: Primary data were collected through personal interaction, interview and discussion with the consumers and other related agencies. The secondary data were collected from important publication and report (published as well as unpublished) from various organizations and agency functioning in the state.

Sample size and sampling: The study covered Bishenpur and Kangpokpi District of Manipur. With the help of Multistage Random Sampling Method, initially sample area were divided into two (2) Districts, followed by each two (2) blocks from the selected districts, i.e. Saitu and Saikul blocks in Kangpokpi and Bishenpur and Moirang blocks in Bishendpur District, and in the third stage the selected blocks were segregated into 16 villages each and finally, with the help of convenient sampling method 160 numbers of respondents were selected for the study (5 × 32 = 160).

Table 13.1: Determination of sample size

Area	District	No. of Blocks	No. of Villages	Total Respondents (No. of respondents, 5 each in the village × No. of villages)	Total
Valley	Beshenpur	2	16	5 × 16 = 80	160
Hill	Kangpokpi	2	16	5 × 16 = 80	
Hill	Kangpokpi	2	16	5 × 16 = 80	
Total		**4**	**32**	**160**	**160**

Data Analysis: The collected primary were tabulated and analysed with the help statistical tools. Initially data collected were gathered, codified and then administered by using percentage method for data analysis. The categorical distribution of the respondent's source of buying behaviour in rural market, implication of bandhs and blockades was calculated. Finally, conclusion is derived by calculating Karl Pearson correlation coefficient analysis to predict the relationship between consumer buying behaviour during bandhs and blockades.

Data Analysis and Interpretation

Two suitable statistical tools, namely Correlation and Percentage Method under SPSS 21.0 version were administered as follows:

(A) Partial Correlation Analysis

Table 13.2: Composite Demographic Characteristics of the Respondents (n=160)

Variables		Gender		Total
		Male	Female	
Age	Below 25 25-35 35-45 Above 45	3 3 8 1	20 43 42 30	23 56 50 31
Education	Illiterate Can only read Can read and write Primary High School Others	0 0 2 9 4 0	30 10 61 34 4 2	30 14 63 43 8 2
Marital Status	Married Un-Married Widow	15 0 0	111 14 20	126 14 20
Mode of purchase	Daily Weekly Monthly Annually	0 2 5 0	63 70 20 0	63 72 25 0

Source: Computed from primary data.

The above Table 13.1 reveals the demographic feature of the study area. There are altogether 160 number of the respondents, out of which 145 respondents belong to female category and the remaining only 15 numbers of respondents were male. 56 female respondents under the age group of 25-35 years were the leading participants in this study. Followed by 50, 31 and 23 under the age group of 35-45 years, above 45 years and below 25 years stood second, third and fifth respectively.

In regard to educational qualification of the respondents, 63 respondents can read and write in the study area which has the highest number of respondents. Followed by 43; 30; 14; 8; and

2 respondents who is in primary level, illiterate, can read only, high school and others stood second, third, fourth, fifth and sixth respectively.

Regarding marital status in the study, 111 respondents were married female, 20 respondents were under the categories belong to widow and only 14 respondents were unmarried. All the male respondents were married in the study area.

The Table also reveal the mode of purchase of essential commodities in the rural market during bandhs and blockade. There are altogether 160 respondents, out of which 72 respondents were purchasing essential commodities on weekly basis in any situation of market. The remaining respondents 63 and 25 purchased the products on daily and monthly basis respectively, in the rural market during bandhs and blockades.

Table 13.3: Frequencies Cross Tabulation of Changing Price of Commodities and No. of Bandhs and Blockades, (N = 160)

Particular		Frequ-ency	Per-centage	Cumulate percentage
Changing price essential commodities during bandhs and blockades	Rs. 5-20	75	46.87	46.87
	Rs. 21-35	11	6.87	53.74
	Rs. 36-50	43	26.87	80.61
	Rs. 50 above	31	19.37	100
	Total	**160**	**100**	
Frequency of bandhs and blockades	1-60 days	137	82.5	82.5
	60-120 days	23	17.5	100
	Total	**160**	**100**	

Source: Computed from the primary data.

In the above Table 13.2 showcases the cross frequency above the changing price of essential commodities and the Number of Bandhs and Blockades in the rural market. There are all together 160 respondents, out of which 75 (46.87%) number of respondents response that the price of essential commodities change at the range of Rs. 5-20 during bandhs and blockades. Followed by 43,31 and

11 respondents with 26.87 per cent, 19.37 per cent and 6.87 per cent stood second, third, and fourth respectively.

The Table above also shows above the frequent occurrence of bandhs and blockades in the study area. Out of the total of 160 respondents, 137 (82.5%) respondents were response that there were at least 1-60 days of bandhs and blockades in the rural market annually. 23 (17.5%) respondents also response that in annually in the rural market, there used to be bandhs and blockade at the range of 60-120 days which interrupt the normalcy of business transaction.

Table 13.4: Partial Correlation between purchase interval, frequency of bandhs and blockades, changing consumption pattern, and changing price of essential commodities

Particular	Purchase interval	Frequency of Bandhs and Blockades	Changing Consumption Pattern	Changing price of commodity
Purchase interval	-			
Frequency of Bandhs and blockades	.758 (.000)			
Changing consumption pattern	.569 (.000)	.487 (.000)		
Changing price of commodities	0.289 (.000)	.526 (.000)	.213 (0.145)	

Source: Computed from primary data.

The above Table 13.3 shows the relationship between price interval of essential commodities, frequency of bandhs and blockades, changing consumption pattern, and changing price of essential commodities in the rural market during bandhs and blockades. The Table revealed that there is strong positive relationship between frequency of bandhs and blockades and the mode of purchase of essential commodities in the rural market (X^2 = 0.758, P = 0.000), moderate positive relationship between changing consumption pattern and mode of purchase of essential commodities (X^2 = 0.569, P = 0.000). The table further revealed the weak positive relationship between the changing price of essential commodities and mode of purchase of essential commodities (X^2 = 0.289, P = 0.000).

The Table also determines the correlation between the variables in the study area. It shows that there is weak positive relation between the consumption pattern and the frequency of bandhs and blockades as the calculated X value shows just 0.487 and P = 0.000. It further maintained that the changing price of essential commodities and the frequency of bandhs and blockades shows average positive relation as the calculated value of X is 0.525, P= 0.000. Last but not the least, there is very weak relationship between changing price of essential commodities and consumption pattern of the study area as the calculated value of X is 0.213, P = 0.145.

Findings

1. It was found that 72 numbers of local consumers purchased essential commodities on weekly basis during bandhs and blockades in rural market. The remaining respondents 63 and 25 of local consumers purchased essential products on daily and monthly basis respectively, in the rural market during bandhs and blockades.
2. No local consumer purchased the essential commodities on annual basis.
3. It was found that there was not much effect of bandhs and blockades on consumption pattern of local consumers as the calculated value of X shows just only 0.487 P = 0.00.
4. It was also found that there is very weak impact of changing price of essential commodities on changing consumption pattern of local consumers (X = 0.213, P = 0.000).
5. It was found that there is strong impact of bandhs and blockades and purchase interval of essential commodities in rural market as calculated value of X shows 0.758.

6. It was seen that there is average impact of frequency of bandhs and blockades on changing price of essential commodities (X = 0.485, P = 0.000).
7. It was also found that there is average impact of purchase interval of essential commodities on changing price of essential commodities (X = 0.525, P = 000).

Finding based on Hypotheses

To sum up there is progressive relationship between bandhs and blockade and buying behaviour of rural consumers, since the calculated value of X shows 0.758, strong positive correlation between the variables. Meaning which the study accepted the alternative hypothesis and rejected null hypothesis.

Suggestions

State government should bring new mechanism to reconcile all the stakeholders for real time emerging of the economy.

It is suggested that, the respondents should purchase the required essential commodity to be sufficient for a month in apprehension on impact of the frequent Economic block in the market.

As far as to the respondents preferences on buying essential commodity is concerned, marketers should evaluate the respondents' response with effect to normal service and during the time of economic blockage in the market and accordingly arrange the required stocks for the better sale for the better smile.

Conclusion

Understanding the negative impacts of bandhs and blockades on the economy of state from many sources like journal, newspaper, TV and Radio, most of the people and many organization have been using bandhs and blockades as effective tools for exerting pressure on the government. Therefore, government needs suitable deliberation to monitor the state economy and to bring early solution of the problems. There is beauty of leaning on role play by the civil organization in state of Mizoram, which becomes driving force on emerging of their economy, golden piece from neighbouring state. Therefore, as much as the stakeholders are coordinate and deliberate on capacity building, there is only losing the tap of state economic health and the end of the day most vulnerable will solely on people of the state.

References

Abdul, G. (2016). Bandh has no Future; Why the Manipuris should stop Bandhs/blockades culture. *A daily English Eveninger*. Retrieved from www.imphaltimes.com

Banga, G. *et al.* (2009). The pre-own car market purchase behaviour and satisfaction of the customer toward Maruti true value. *Indian Marketing Journal.* Vol. 39, issue 1, January, pp. 92-101.

Bimola, K. (2017). Impact of economic blockades and demonetisation in Manipur. *The people chronicle.* Retrieved from www.thepeoplechronicle.in

Hanagandi, R.K. (2010). Customer Satisfaction in response to select Washing Machine brand—An Empirical Study. *Journal of Commerce and Management thought.* Vol. 6, issue 4, April, pp. 116-131.

Indian Oil Corporation Limited (2009). *Petroleum product (POL): Supply and Distribution in Manipur. Souvenir Consumer club of Manipur.* Vol. 8, pp. 16-19.

Kumar, D.N.S. (2008).Changing consumer behaviour and soft drinks marketing in North-Goa: A case study. *Indian Journal of Marketing.* Vol. 38, issue 10. Oct., pp. 37-49.

Nagaraja, B. (2004). Consumer behaviour in Rural Area: A micro level study on buying behaviour of rural consumer in Kavali Mandal. *Indian Journal of Marketing.* pp. 31-37.

Pathak, S.V. and Tripathi, A.P. (2009). Customer Shopping Behaviour among Modern retail format: A Study of Delhi and NCR. *Indian Journal of Marketing.* Vol. 39, issue 2, Feb., pp. 3-14.

Rahman, J. (2014). *Economic implication of intra-state conflict: evidence from state.* Retrieved from www.jism.net.in

Ramanathan, V. and Hari, K. (2011). A study on consumer perceptions about organized *versus* unorganized retailer at Kanchipuram, Tamil Nadu. *Indian Journal of Marketing.* Vol. 8, issue 28, Dec. pp. 11-23.

Sharma, S.K., (2014). *Dynamic of Bandhs and Blockades in Northeast India: A case study of Manipur and the way ahead.* Retrieved from www.claws.in.> images > publication_pdf

Singh, A.M. (2007). The growing trend of Bandhs and Blockades in Manipur. Institute for Defence Studies and Analysis. Retrieved from www.idsa.in

Singh, Ch. N. (2009). Toward new perspective of consumer movement in Manipur. *Souvenir Consumer Club Manipur*. Vol 8, pp. 1-6.

Singh, L.R. (2009). Educational Institutions and Consumer Protection Act, 1986. *Souvenir Consumer Club Manipur.* Vol. 8, pp. 8-14.

Turner, K. and Krizik, R.L. (2006). A Meaning—Centre Approach to Customer Satisfaction. *Management Communication Quarterly*. Vol. 20, No. 2, November, pp. 115-147.

14

Role of Education in Consumer Awareness

Thangminlun Singsit

Introduction

Everyone of us is a consumer and therefore, has the right to consumer education. But, it is the right education that would facilitate us to act as an informed consumer, throughout one's life. One of the problems of the Indian consumers is their ignorance. Most of the consumers are apathetic because they are not aware of their rights. Then, they do not have the strength to resist whenever they are cheated or exploited and they suffer silently. It is for this reason that education should be given to each and everyone of them.

From the period of Vedas, Dharma Shastras and kingdoms itself there were many norms, conditions and prescribed code of conduct for the traders against the exploitation of consumers. In the barter system the people with abundant resources used to exploit the needy. Few customers want to show their social status by purchasing the expensive products. Till the origin of marketing concept marketer is the king. But the consumerism started as a revolution almost all the marketers became customer centric and the speed of inventions and their usage increased. Today, consumer is the king of the market. He is now at the centre stage of all market activities in the economy. However, with the advancement in technology, education, impact of globalization and changing expectations of consumers the business men are adopting various strategies to earn profit at the cost of the customer in order to meet the increasing competition. Every business revolves around the customer and customer is also the only person subjected to all types of exploitation. In spite of various consumer laws and measures consumers are still being exploited and the main reason is lack of awareness among the consumers about their rights and protection measures.

Education is one of the important factors which brought liberalization from exploitation, ignorance, superstition and so on. It enlightens individuals and causes growth of the economy. It is true that in this developed trade and global market consumer is the ruler. But it is a pity that the consumer is being exploited in many ways. It is evident that the increased literacy rate will reduce the exploitation. Consumer education is taking place in many ways. The Government and educational institutions have identified the importance of consumer education and giving support in many ways.

Consumer education is basically an education which brings about behavioural changes in a person who goes to the market to buy. It is the process of gaining the knowledge and skills needed in managing consumer resources and taking actions to influence the factors which affect consumer decisions. The need for consumer education has increased over time as today the consumers operate in an increasingly complex marketplace and are faced with increasing amounts of information and an expanding choice of complex products and services. As a consequence they are more exposed to fraud and require a wider range of skills and knowledge than ever before. Consumer education is a potent tool for empowering consumers as it equips consumers with information and skills necessary to meet challenges posed by the markets. Through education, consumer obtains information about the products and the services and empower them and make them aware of their rights and responsibilities and helps to ensure their welfare.

Literature Review

Akram, S. (1994) despicts that consumerism in our country has not yet reached the take off stage. A large number of Indian consumers are poor, illiterate, ill-informed and unorganised. In order to check this unhappy state of affairs, it is important to educate the consumers about their rights.

According to Rama Rao (1984), the consumer himself is partly responsible for exploitation, since he is unaware of his rights. Majority of the Indian Consumers have remained unprotected because they are being apathetic ignorant non-price conscious, irrational, food of bargaining without information about product quality etc., have remained unprotected. The main reason for such a state of affairs is lack of education and rational thinking among consumers.

According to Aziah Hashim *et al.*, (2002), consumer education is a means of providing knowledge to consumers so that the individual consumer would be able to develop or acquire the skills, aptitude and values needed to become a responsible and responsive consumer in market place as well as in the society.

C.S. Rayudu (1983) stated that the consumer should have knowledge on wide fields of mercantile practices like legal protection available, exaggerated advertisements, price variations, substitutes, fair and unfair practices, short weights and measures and price policies of Government. But the percentage of literacy is very low in our country. He opined that consumer co-operative societies can be an effective instrument of consumer resistance against the exploitation.

Fazal & Singh (1991) stated that consumer education has four suspects which are related to four core reasons why consumer education is needed. They are Informed choice (consumer must have knowledge about goods and services by learning and getting more information about it), Value System (Consumers must learn how to share and care as consumer are part of the society, Recognition of Responsibilities and Rights (there are three distinctive roles, as workers, consumers and citizens). It is important to articulate and understand both responsibilities as well as rights as consumers) and Catalyst for Action (Consumer education must catalyze action. They must become aware of the available avenues of consumer complaint and redress and learn to use them for their benefit).

Rebello (1991) cautioned that unless the consumers continue being alert and interested in protecting their interests, businessmen, traders and advertisers would once again become immersed in themselves and forget their consumers.

Nageshwar Rao (1990) stated that consumer education makes the consumers as responsible citizens and demand value for the money paid, quality, service and satisfaction. It safeguards people against exploitation.

Narayanaswamy (1992) concludes in his study that once consumers become more knowledgeable they can easily resist any anti-consumer move besides being wise and prudent in their money management.

Objectives of the Study

1. To find out the most important target of consumer education.
2. To identify the need for introducing consumer education in the basic curriculum of the education system.
3. To assess the effectiveness of educational institutions, Government and NGOs in educating consumers.

Research Methodology

The information obtained from secondary data and the study is exploratory in nature. The data are collection of several articles, journals and presentations related to consumer education, consumerism and role of education in consumer awareness through which the analysis and discussions are carried out.

Analysis and Discussion

The process of development along with the expanding globalisation and liberalization process has increased the number of consumer related issues. Consumer protection has earned an important place in the political, economic and social agendas of many nations. In India, the Government has taken many steps including legislative, to protect consumers. However, this is largely unknown to many citizens irrespective of whether they are educated or uneducated. With an enormous population along with high level of poverty, unemployment and poor literacy level, consumer awareness continues to remain low. With the increasing changes in economic conditions, the children especially are becoming young consumers at an early age. Children must learn to obtain information about goods and services, understand the psychology of selling and advertising, learn to shop wisely and distinguish between wants and needs. They must also understand the alternatives of conserving and saving rather than buying and consuming.

Almost all countries acknowledge that children and young people are particularly important targets of consumer education as these age groups account for an ever-increasing share of family consumption. At the same time they are likely to be particularly vulnerable to making unwise decisions and falling victim to aggressive marketing. Children are spending more of their leisure time watching television at the cost of other pursuits such as reading or sports. With the introduction of a number of specialized satellite channels, television enjoys a large viewership base consisting of children. Exposure to the marketplace as young shoppers has made most children aware of the different kinds of products that are available. A majority of the advertisements are aimed at young children today, especially those covering food products, beverages and cosmetics (especially toothpaste/fairness creams). Advertising influences the food preferences and eating habits of children to a large extent. Unfortunately, many advertisements make false promises, are highly exaggerated and give incomplete descriptions of products. The media, schools and parents along with consumer groups need to help children develop the ability to understand the purpose of advertising. There is so much more information available to children that they must perceive the importance of distinguishing between different sources of information.

The consumption patterns are changing fast and children today are very clear on their choices regarding food, clothing, cosmetics or accessories. Parents are increasingly permitting their children to take decisions when shopping. It then becomes very important for children to check details (for example labels) before buying products. Children can be taught to shop wisely and a few precautions will ensure that they choose the right product at the right price.

The fact that both parents often work outside the home has led to a change in the role of parents in consumer training. With this in mind, many countries have made consumer education compulsory in primary, secondary and in some countries in upper-secondary grades. The objectives include helping pupils to gain knowledge of what it means to act as informed consumers; develop and understand society's functions as a whole and specific role of consumers; master skills to function as informed consumer. The ultimate goal is for consumers to act spontaneously in informed, educated and responsible way. In most countries, consumer education is integrated into the school curriculum in an interdisciplinary way. Subjects that may include consumer concepts are economics, mathematics, biology, chemistry, language, arts, business education and home economics. These subjects cover a variety of issues which are important for consumers in contemporary society, including the effects of consumption on the environment, production and consumption in a global perspective, health and food, product quality and safety, and financial management. Relevant issues are thus addressed in cross-curricular themes such as home economics, citizenship, civic education or social studies. Consumer education also involves environmental education as it deals with the importance of conserving (natural resources) and sustaining (recycling and reusing) the environment, including the direct health effects of environmental pollution and toxic products on consumers. Schools must incorporate consumer education into school's curricula as it is important to impart the practical skills and critical ability needed to cope with social and economic changes.

It is in school that civic awareness is shaped and schools are fertile ground for moulding the mind of future consumers. There is no doubt that the integration of consumer education into the formal school curriculum can be of immense benefit to societies. Students already make consumer choices in school cafeterias, canteens and local shops. Students for example should be educated to distinguish need from wants, to budget their spending and to make informed choices about the goods they buy. Surely, the growing market products, services and advertising aimed at the young consumers makes consumer education in the formal schools all the more necessary.

In addition, a variety of non-formal education tools or activities (i.e. not included in the curriculum) complement more traditional methods. These are websites, videos, exercise books, school magazines as well as theme days, school competitions and contests, consumer clubs, national fairs for teachers and pupils and special educational programmes. These non-formal teaching tools are mostly produced by consumer associations in co-operation with parent-teacher associations, and in some countries with other stakeholders. Consumer education generally focuses on the primary and secondary school curriculum. However, in some countries it also takes place in universities.

Role of Educational Institution in Educating Consumers

Consumer awareness and education surely avoids exploitation. As it is included by majority of the universities in their syllabus whether the students are interested or not they are taught. Not only consumerism it is evident that all development comes through education. Once there is growth in the literacy automatically there will be growth in all fields of the economy. The immense competition and technological development brought high impact on the quality of the goods. The developments in the media got the information to the people. But it is fact that the public are still victims of the marketers because of unscrupulous and exploitative trade practices.

- Consumer protection is identified as a significant factor by the schools and universities. The Central Board of Secondary Education has highlighted the guiding points of consumer protection and IGNO University has introduced a special course for both under graduate and post graduate students.
- Few schemes are under finalization for setting up National level projects in collaboration with leading consumer organizations, industry associations and academic institutions like IITs, IIMs, IIPA, IIFT and reputed Central Universities to provide consumer education, training and research on a more structured and sustained basis.
- A Centre of Excellence is established by reputed organizations like IITs and IIMs to facilitate action suits for major consumer problems.
- Many schools, colleges and Universities are actively taking part in various schemes introduced by the government. Ex: *Grahak Jagaran.*
- A scheme was launched in 2002 to set up consumer club in each Middle/High/Higher Secondary School/College affiliated to a government recognized Board/University.
- Bureau of Indian Standards organizes education utilization of standards programmes in various educational institutes.
- Some reputed institutes like VIT University and IITs have courses like Indian Business Environment, Consumerism, and Consumer Protection. These institutes are also conducting various campaigns in and around the University surroundings and are also doing many projects regarding Consumer awareness through which they are in a position to analyze the sort of approach that people are expecting from the campaigns.

- Seminars, conferences, workshops, consumer festivals, research/evaluation studies are encouraged by various grants and the results are being published in the form of books, monographs and pamphlets on consumer education and awareness. The Indian Institute of Public Administration (IIPA), New Delhi, has been identified as the nodal organization to administer this scheme. Till March 2006, 291 applications were received and 95 applicants have been recommended for sanction of grant. IIPA conducted a five-day workshop on 'consumer protection and consumer welfare' for the faculty of various educational institutes with an intention to create resource persons.
- A National Consumer Helpline project has been established in coordination with Delhi University, Department of Commerce on 15-3-2005. Consumers from all over the country can dial toll free number 1800-11-4000 and seek telephonic counselling for consumer problems. Maximum calls received from this Helpline is found to be related to telecom, courier, banking, insurance, financial services etc. On an average 6000-7000 calls are received every month by the NCH from more than 25 States and Union Territories.

Role of Government in Educating Consumers

The government has implemented a number of Consumer Laws and serious measures for the protection of consumer against unfair trade practices. The Consumer Protection Act is a compassionate social legislation that provides for protection of rights of the consumers and redressal of consumer disputes through the three tier quasi-judicial consumer dispute redressal mechanism at district, state and national level. Further, the Department of Consumer Affairs, Government of India, has introduced a number of schemes for spreading awareness among the Consumers and also educating them about their rights as provided in the Consumer Protection Act, 1986. The Department of Consumer Affairs has been assigned the prime responsibility of consumer education, protection and monitoring the prices and availability of essential commodities. The Department has launched a publicity campaign to create consumer awareness and strengthen the consumer protection mechanism. The other initiatives taken by the Department include:

- Computerization and computer networking of consumer fora.
- Strengthening Consumer Fora.
- National Consumer Helpline.
- Consumer On-line Research and Empowerment Centre.
- Gold hallmarking.
- Regulating future markets.
- Setting up of consumer clubs.
- Strengthening of weight and measurement organizations.
- Comparative testing of products.
- Laying down of standards through Bureau of Indian Standards.

However, the institutions of higher learning, particularly the research institutions and the universities have remained untouched by these schemes. There is no doubt that these institutions can play a meaningful role in creating awareness and also educating the young consumers about their rights and obligations as well as to fill the gap in terms of research studies in the area of consumer protection and consumer welfare. Therefore, the Department of Consumer Affairs, Government of India has launched a scheme to promote the involvement of Research Institutions, Universities and Colleges in consumer protection and consumer welfare. Under the Scheme, grant will be sanctioned by the Indian Institute of Public Administration, New Delhi from the Consumer Welfare Fund to the Research Institutions, Universities and Colleges for undertaking research projects and the amount of grant will vary as per the requirement of the project, within the ceiling of Rs. 3.00 to 5.00 lakh per research project. The Scheme does not cover expenditure on basic infrastructure, building, foreign travel and purchase of major equipment.

Role of NGOs in Educating Consumers

The role of Non-government Organizations has long been recognized as being of importance in the development of low income settlement and providing support for income generation. Non-government Organizations have multiple and varied approaches to reducing urban poverty. In some circumstances Non-government Organizations work directly with educating women and make aware about their rights. Non-government Organizations provide important services throughout the world. Their scope covers a wide spectrum of services such as health and welfare, research, education, social organizations and professional associations. A number of initiatives have already been launched by the Non-government Organizations. Many of them have been successful, however, most of these initiatives are small in nature and local in context.

Various consumer organizations and non-governmental organizations set up for non-profit motive have a strong role in promoting the interests of the consumers. It can be summed up as under:

(i) Educating the general public about consumer rights by organizing training programmes, seminars and workshops.
(ii) Publishing periodicals and other publications to impart knowledge about consumer problems, legal reporting, reliefs available and other matter of interest.
(iii) Carrying out comparative testing of consumer products in accredited laboratories to test qualities, brands etc.
(iv) Encouraging consumers to strongly protest and take an action against unscrupulous, exploitative and unfair trade practices of sellers.
(v) Providing legal assistance to consumers by way of providing aid, legal advice etc.

(vi) Filing complaints in appropriate consumer courts on behalf of consumers.

(vii) Taking an initiative in filing cases in consumer courts in the interest of general public, not for any individual.

Some important consumer organisation and NGOs operating in India:

1. Consumer Coordination Council, Delhi.
2. Common Cause, Delhi.
3. Voluntary Organisation in Interest of Consumer Education (VOICE), Delhi.
4. Consumer Education and Research Centre (CERC), Ahmadabad.
5. Consumers' Association, Kolkata.

The first organization to really make an impact was the Consumer Management Society of India (CGSI), Bombay, started by nine housewives in 1966 with Mrs. Leela Jog as its founder secretary. Instead of just holding conferences and meetings and asking questions like earlier consumer associations, it started testing and reporting the quality of items of daily use of harvest and behaviour consumer complaints. It has 8 branches at various places carrying on exposure, exhibitions and education. It publishes a magazine called 'keemat', in English, for consumer information.

Another organization which finished a significant contribution to the root of consumers is the Consumer Education and Research Centre (CERC) which started in Ahmadabad in 1978. It added a new dimension to the Consumer movement with Prof. Manubhai Shah, the Managing Trustee CERC. The organization constantly used legal machinery to carry about changes and protect consumer human rights. Its special focus and intervention is beside the governments and public corporations. It has a big library, computer centre and a product testing laboratory. Recently, it also launched a project on comparative testing in Ahmadabad, where comparative testing, ranking and evaluation of consumer products are being undertaken with the aim of publication of such findings for consumer education. To begin with, testing of food, pharmaceuticals and domestic appliances have started. Findings will be published and action may be initiated against unsafe products. CERC also undertakes internship training for any consumer organization, besides routine exhibitions, seminars and publications of the magazine '*Consumer Confrontation*'.

Findings

- It is learnt that children and young people are the most targeted consumer group, likely to be particularly vulnerable to making unwise decisions and falling victims to aggressive marketing.
- The study highlights the fact that introduction/imparting of consumer education in schools and colleges would mean an earlier preparation of children and young people as an informed, educated and responsible consumer.
- Educational institutions are impressively performing their part in imparting consumer education through seminars, workshops, conferences, research etc. and thus, educational institutions are found to be the best media for educating consumers.
- The governments besides providing legal protection to the consumers takes up various initiatives, launched publicity campaigns and sanction schemes for promoting and imparting consumer education.
- Various consumer organizations and Non-Governmental Organizations are actively participating in providing various services related to consumer protection and welfare and in educating consumers such as health and welfare, research, education, social organizations and professional associations.

Suggestions

- Educational institutions should widen their area of participation in consumer education. They can start many campaigns and create awareness not only among the students but also among the rural, urban, tribal and even among the illiterates.

- To extent and expand the existing programmes, schemes and activities granted by Government, consumer organisations and NGOs should reach out to every nook and corner of the nation.
- Seminars, workshops, discussions should be frequently conducted in the educational institutions. Books on consumer protection, magazines, reports, pamphlets, cassettes, CDs, slides should be available in all libraries.
- Consumer education can be made more relevant by linking to different situations such as at school, at home, while in public place etc. Parent's education programmes and family support programmes can help parents in good decisions making on behalf of their wards.
- Government should encourage consumer organisations and other interested groups, including the media, to undertake education and information programmes, particularly for the benefit of low-income consumer groups in rural and urban areas.

Conclusion

Education is considered to be the most effective tool in imparting consumer awareness. To educate the present generation about Consumer Protection Act, consumer forums, agencies and courts, educational institutes have to play a vital role. The use of various educational tools, such as seminars, workshops, conferences, discussions, campaigns by educational institutions, NGOs, governments and consumer organisations serve as an effective tool in imparting consumer education and thus, consumer can be aware of their rights and responsibilities. The active involvement and participation from all quarters, i.e. the Central and State Governments, educational institutions, the NGOs, the print and electronic media, is the more needed role in educating consumers.

References

Akram, S. (1994). Consumer Protection in India under the shadow of Legislation, The *Indian Journal of Commerce*, Vol. XXXXVIII, No. 181, December.

Andrey Rebello (1991). *Societal Response to Consumer Movement*, Ahmedabad: Consumer Education and Research Society.

Aziah, H., Nurizan, Y., Naimah, M.S., & Jariah, M. (2002). Concept of consumer education in Malaysia, *International Journal of Consumer Studies*, 3(Mar), 77.

Consumer awareness at school level, *The Hindu*, Tuesday, April 16, 2002.

Dzulkarnain Mazlan, Ahmad Md. Redzuan, Darussalam Abu Bakar, (2014). *Consumer Education in Creating a Consumer Conscious Nation.*

Fazal, A. & Singh, B. (1991). *Consumer education: A resource handbook.* Penang: International Organization of Consumer Unions.

Nageshwar Rao, S., (1990). Consumer Education in Villages, *Indian Journal of Marketing.* April.

Narayanaswamy (1992). Education: A tool for Consumer Protection, *Consumer Confrontation.* May-June.

Pulidindi Venugopal, P. Vijayakumar, M. Varun Kumar (2012). *Consumer Awareness and Role of Educational Institutions.*

P. Uma Maheswari Devi, B. Sankara Rao (2016). *Consumer Protection Awareness —Role of Education.*

Rama Rao, P.V.S. (1984). Consumer Protection—Myth or Reality? *Indian Journal of Marketing*, Vol. XIV, No. 7, March.

Rayudu, C.S. (1983). Consumer Movement in India, *Indian Journal of Marketing*, Vol. XVI, Nos. 1-2, September-October.

Shodhganga.inflibnet.ac.in.

Index